"The title of this book by Edith Vilamajó, *Formation for Transformation*, points to something that should be every educator's ideal. This subject is especially important for those who contribute to educational work in evangelical churches, where, for better or for worse, there is an ongoing educational process. Those who currently minister in these churches have often prepared for the task by completing some sort of theological education. Through critical reflection, and based on her own experience as a Christian educator, the author of this book applies her pedagogical training to assess both evangelical theological education and the educational work of churches in Spain. Vilamajó offers a valuable overview of the process of pedagogical reflection. What she proposes in this book will be of great help to those who teach, but at the same time she strives to evaluate and improve that teaching."

**Samuel Escobar**, Doctor in Philosophy and Educational Sciences, Complutense University of Madrid, and leading theologian, missiologist, and author.

"The current global landscape – with millions of people displaced due to violence, hunger, and climate change, and with socio-political crises at every turn – demands a response from those who identify themselves as followers of Jesus Christ. It is what makes the question at the heart of this profound and powerful book so urgent: What type of training will transform these people into agents responsible for God's plan of restoration for His world? The author offers valuable theological clues and practical tools for constructing integral processes for communal learning that are marked by an encounter with God through His Word, opening up to the work of the Holy Spirit, and the search for a transformed way of living in the world. A resource that is not to be missed!"

**Ruth Padilla De Borst**, President of the Community of Interdisciplinary Theological Studies (CETI in Spanish).

"It brings me great joy to see *Formation for Transformation* by Edith Vilamajó in print. We were greatly in need of a thought-provoking look at our training and teaching models. As the author says, 'The fact that a teacher has taught does not necessarily mean that a student has learned'. The starting point of this book is an in-depth look at the biblical basis for transformation, but it is also very practical. The questions that are regularly interspersed throughout the book provide food for thought and make this a handbook that can accompany us through the process of transformation – a process that is no longer only for our students, but also for ourselves as teachers. As Edith herself puts it, '[God] has so much more in store for us!'."

**Andrés Reid**, Director of the Evangelical School of Theology, Spain.

"The book you hold in your hands is the result of a teacher's passionate life journey – a teacher who believes in the active and effective power of education. It is a book that goes beyond empirical research. *Formation for Transformation* changes us, provokes us, and motivates us to be better teachers. Vilamajó writes from the heart and captivates with her simple and straightforward language. In a delicate and humble way that combines theory and experience, her reading takes us on an inward-looking journey to rediscover and identify ourselves as teachers, with shared fears, weaknesses, and frustrations. By the end, she takes us by the hand as we long to emerge, to take that vital breath of fresh air, to better ourselves, and she leads us through the process of drawing nearer to and becoming more like the Teacher of teachers.
This is an intentional, provocative, challenging, and essential book for all those of us who are engaged in biblical and theological teaching."

**Jesús Caramés**, Rector of the Faculty of Theology of the Assemblies of God.

"This is a book the author was destined to write. After dedicating a long period of her life to training university students and the team of workers at GBU and IFES Europe, she has lifted her sights in order to help the Church and theological seminaries think about what kind of training transforms people's lives so that they can become more like Jesus. This book is intended to stimulate our imagination and prompt us to change the way we teach Scriptures. Her own approach is already different, with questions that make the reader play a leading role in their own formation."

**Jaume Llenas**, Staff worker for GBU Spain and Co-ordinator of the Lausanne Movement in Spain.

"There is no doubt that there is an education crisis going on, and not just within the evangelical world. Edith Vilamajó broaches the subject based on careful analysis and reaches very practical and manageable conclusions. This is not just a book; it is a veritable gold mine, a didactical handbook that has the potential to completely change a ministry for the better. Rather than simply read it, I would recommend studying this book – a book that anyone who works in ministry should get their hands on."

**José Hutter**, President of the theology work group of the Evangelical Alliance of Spain.

"I have in my hands a book that will allow us to carry out a serious and necessary review of our spiritual formation system. Edith explores the basic elements that any Christian who is passionate about teaching should consider, challenging the generalised practices of our time, which reduce training to merely transmitting information, and she encourages us to position ourselves so that only His grace will transform us."

**Rubén Gómez Cuenca**, Advisor on planting Christian communities and on spiritual formation from an organic missional paradigm.

# Formation for Transformation

## Series Preface

While we delight to serve the academic community, our mission is to enable the global church to engage more readily in God's mission in its very diverse contexts. To do this we seek to bring practitioners and academics together. Our desire is that this series will bridge the gap that sometimes exists between, on the one hand, Christian leaders and mission practitioners and, on the other, Christian researchers.

## About the Author

Edith Vilamajó Sanchis studied Pedagogy at the University of Barcelona and then completed a Master's in Theology at Trinity Evangelical Divinity School (USA). She dedicated the first twenty years of her ministry to working with students. The first stage was with GBU in Spain (1996-2002) and during the second stage she worked with IFES Europe (2003-2014), which included several visits to Latin America. In 2016, she received a Doctor of Ministry degree in Transformational Leadership from Ashland Theological Seminary (USA).

Since then, she mentors people who are mainly involved in ministry. She is also a Professor and the Dean of Students at the FIEIDE Evangelical School of Theology (EET) in Spain. She lives in Oxford with her husband Peter and son Alex.

# Formation for Transformation

## An Approach to Renewing the Teaching Ministry within the Church

Edith Vilamajó Sanchis

Originally published in Spanish 2019 as
*Formar para transformar. Propuesta para renovar el ministerio de enseñanza en la Iglesia*
in Barcelona by Andamio Editorial

First English edition published 2022 by Regnum Books International

Translated from the original Spanish by Rebecca Breekveldt

Regnum is an imprint of the Oxford Centre for Mission Studies
St. Philip and St. James Church, Woodstock Road
Oxford, OX2 6HR, UK
www.regnumbooks.net

09 08 07 06 05 04 03 8 7 6 5 4 3 2 1



**British Library Cataloguing in Publication Data**
A catalogue record for this book is available from the British Library

ISBN: 978-1-5064-9744-0
eBook ISBN: 978-1-5064-9745-7

Typeset by Words by Design

Cover image by Earl Wilcox www.unsplash.com

Distributed by Fortress Press in the US, Canada, India, and Brazil

Dedicated to Papá and Maman:

I first saw passion for teaching in you.

Also, you nurtured my vocation.

To my son Alexandre Martin Guy:

You are my best student, but above all,

my best teacher.

And we all, who with unveiled faces contemplate the Lord's glory, are being transformed into his image with ever-increasing glory, which comes from the Lord, who is the Spirit. 2 Corinthians 3:18

# Contents

# Acknowledgements

I have had, and continue to have, the privilege of being surrounded by many people who have been an enormous blessing. This book would not have seen the light of day if it were not for the multitude of people who, in one way or another, have been or are part of my own transformation process to become more like Jesus.

This book is partly the result of my doctoral thesis, which I presented in 2016 at Ashland Theological Seminary. My time at Ashland (from January 2013 to November 2014), writing my doctoral dissertation, was one of the most important turning points in my life. That research period not only gave me the chance to articulate some of the things I had been considering for some time, but also allowed me to experience the healing work God carried out in me. I want to thank Norman Bowman once more, who lovingly but firmly encouraged me to consider a sabbatical and who enabled all the practical steps so I could go to Ashland. I want to also thank IFES (International Fellowship of Evangelical Students) and GBU (IFES' Spanish student movement), who not only granted me the privilege of serving with them for two decades, but who also gave me the time to take a sabbatical to rest and be renewed. There are many people who I had the privilege of living alongside in Ashland: staff, professors, students, and friends. I have been very blessed and enriched by all of them. I am grateful to God for Terry Wardle, who has been one of my best and most inspiring professors – a powerful agent in the hands of God on my path towards healing and the academic advisor for my dissertation. I am also thankful for Matt Lewis, who taught me so much, not only through the art of being a good academic professor who is both close and vulnerable with students, but because he offered me the opportunity to "try" teaching in the academic world by letting me be his graduate assistant. I gained so much through our conversations on education. When I grow up, I want to be like these people! And once again, thanks to Belfast Bible College for allowing me to intrude and work with them on my dissertation project.

My first conversations with the publishing house Andamio were with Francisco Mira. It quickly became clear that publishing a doctoral dissertation would not be a good idea, however, he was still willing to work on it. Not only was Francisco the director of the publishing house, but I also consider him to be my spiritual father. I sometimes ask myself whether I would still follow the Lord's path if it weren't for His grace and the presence of Francisco in my life. Furthermore, Francisco believed in this project and gave it a place within a publishing house with a long tradition of publishing quality books that nurture and edify our lives as believers and our churches. I hope my contribution will add to this endeavour. Thanks as well to Sarai Lagos for walking me through the various stages of publishing a book – always with so much enthusiasm and such a great disposition. To Miguel Llop for his painstaking proofreading and apt corrections. To Samuel López and Raquel Arlándiz, "Mr. and Mrs. Wilson", for the fabulous book design. The cover captures an image that has been very meaningful to me since I was a child.

I don't consider myself someone who writes well. I knew that, if I were going to write a book, I would need an editor. I chose the best: Dorcas González Bataller. From the beginning, she told me: "Don't worry. You do your job, writing, and I will do my job, editing". Her professional rigour, alongside a long-time friendship, have made working with her more than a pleasure: a gift.

Virginia Woolf advocated for women having money and a physical place in which to write. God granted me both. Fraser and Rosie Hutchinson opened their home for months, so that I could have a quiet place to write. When their baby was born, I got to enjoy a space in St. James Church – the Anglican church in Cowley, where we live. On top of two large grants from Langham Writers' Grants and Urco Foundation, many people have given donations throughout this time. We have never lacked for anything.

There are many people who have been praying for me and for us during this time and who have checked in every now and then. I know that God has heard each one of those prayers.

There are hundreds of students and workers that I have had the privilege to see transformed, mainly in the context of GBU and IFES, but also through local churches and other ministries. They have been incredible teachers.

While I was writing this book, I put together a course on the same subject for the Evangelical School of Theology (EET in Spanish). Andrés Reid, the school's Director, and Ricard Bardés, the Degree Co-ordinator, have always been enthusiastic about my contribution. My students from this new stage with EET (Isaac Arbalat, Juan Parras, Joaquín Castro, África Ruíz, Samuel Pérez, Luis Aristimuño, Ana María Portillo, and Eva Méndez) were the first to read the contents of this book and they did so with enthusiasm, dedication, a critical eye, and a commitment to helping me find the best paths to teaching-learning that leads to transformation. It has been a joy and privilege to be their teacher. With them, I feel that there is hope of change.

Peter, my dear husband, a gift from God, has walked alongside me and continues to do so. During this stage in our lives, he adjusted his work situation so that we could keep looking after our son, Alex, and I could devote myself to what God has called me to. We do ministry together, as a family. A few days ago, Alex beat me to it and gifted me his first book, written and designed by him. He doesn't yet understand that I have always wanted to dedicate this book to him. My greatest desire is to see him love Jesus, the One who has the power to call and transform him.

It is my hope that this book will be like a fragrant offering to my Lord, my God, my Saviour, and my Healer. "*Soli Deo Gloria*".

# Introduction to the English Translation

I thought it would be helpful to provide a short introduction as readers may wonder why a book like this needs to be translated into English. Are there not enough books on this subject already written and published in English? The world, including myself, has benefitted greatly from the theological thinking of the Western English-speaking world. However, it is imperative that we also hear from other voices. We should all, from one side of the planet to the other, learn from one another. It has been a joy to see the increasing number of writers and books from the Global South being translated and published in English in recent years. I commend Regnum Books for making this a priority and thank them for taking on board the publication of this work. I pray I may add with my contribution.

I am indebted to the wonderful translation done by Rebecca Breekveldt. She has worked with excellence and has captured the spirit of the Spanish text. But, as with all translations, there are words that are almost impossible to translate. I want to highlight one in particular: the Spanish word *formación*. This word, inspired by the verse in Galatians 4:1 "until Christ is formed in you", was adopted years ago in IFES, the ministry I served for 20 years. We believed it encapsulated, better than any other term, what we were trying to do with our students. It provided a holistic concept, wider than education (intellectual level) and wider than training (skill level). When we "form", we partner with God to see those whom we serve made into the image of Christ in every area of life: spiritual, intellectual, physical, emotional, relational, and functional. I am delighted that Regnum has understood my reasoning for using the word "Formation" in the title of this book and invite you to have this explanation of the word in mind every time you read training, teaching, education or other.

Finally, I need to say that the translation of this book into English, in addition to allowing my dear husband and editor to understand it (!), meets one of my profound desires: making it available for the many people I have served alongside over the years who do not read Spanish.

With this book, as I say in the main introduction, I have tried to articulate what I may not have been able to do well enough before. This English translation is especially dedicated to all my colleagues, staff, and students in IFES. Receive it as my “second chance” and my gift. May the Lord continue to equip you to do the amazing work you are doing.

Edith Vilamajó Sanchis

Oxford, November 2021

# Introduction

I was born and called to learn and teach. However, I found formal schooling very difficult, especially at secondary and university level. When I started teaching, within the informal context of a ministry with university students I was involved in, I inevitably repeated what I had mostly seen and experienced: the lecture method. I would painstakingly research and prepare myself, but as time went by, my concern grew. I started asking myself: How do I know whether students are following me when I teach? How do I assess whether students are really learning and applying what they learn? What are my objectives and motivations when I teach? I would reflect on what helped me overcome the academic challenges I had faced so that I could transfer these to my educational practices.

First, I thrived when my teachers showed an interest in me and encouraged me in specific challenges, when they brought out the best in me and believed in me, and when they recognised my efforts, my potential, and my gifts.

Second, when I was instructed by people who were passionate about their subjects and transmitted that passion to me – drawing my attention, respectfully motivating me to participate and ask questions without the threat of looking ridiculous. When it wasn't just about information; they also gave of themselves – both inside the classroom and, on occasion, outside of it. When they shared not only their intellectual knowledge, but also their integrity, commitment, and humility.

Third, when they gave me the chance to participate in activities that went beyond the purely academic. For example, when I acted as class representative both in secondary school and at the seminary, and I had the chance to successfully contribute to the well-being of the student body. These opportunities were very satisfying because I was able to carry out projects that I was enthusiastic and passionate about and develop my leadership skills. On these occasions, I could show that I was more than an academic profile, and I also learned a lot!

Fourth, when I was part of a Christian student association during my days at university – a ministry I later served with for 20 years. The relationships I built there sustained my spiritual life and helped me connect my academic side with my faith in a comprehensive way.

Fifth, when I understood that the subjects did not exist in a vacuum, but that it was important to understand how they were all connected.

Sixth, when I had the chance to explore the different ways of doing academia – through group and individual research projects, group discussions, online forums, study trips, and reading. They opened my eyes to the variety of ways through which we can learn.

All this reflecting led me to focus on matters of methodology and to make myself vulnerable, not just when I teach, but also when I interact with students in informal settings. I wanted to explore different ways of teaching because I realised that effective teaching wasn't simply about brilliant content. Rather, and especially, it is about students really learning. Furthermore, I didn't want to be seen as a distant teacher – I wanted to embody what I was teaching as well as being accessible and sharing life with my students.

Some new questions have come up in recent years: When I teach, how can I touch both hearts and minds? How can I help students position themselves so that they experience real change and how do I evaluate that? What role does the Holy Spirit play and how do I leave room for Him to move?

These questions have led me to believe that, in both theological education and Christian formation in general, the academic side has taken precedence over spiritual and practical formation. As a vocational teacher, if I want to maintain my integrity, I can't make the same mistake of polarising and teaching in that unbalanced way. Those of us who teach within the context of theological education, both formally and informally, or are Christian teachers teaching in various different contexts, should all aspire to integrate academic teaching, spiritual formation, and practical training. This is what lies behind my passion and what has led me to look into this further through my doctoral dissertation and, later, through writing this book.

Besides the reality of my educational background, there is also my ministerial journey. There are moments in life when one stops and thinks: "If only I could start again…". I felt this deeply after a long period of working in ministry: "If only I had been more patient; if only I had explained that better; if only I had communicated with more grace; if only I had been more humble and considered others greater than myself; if only I had believed more firmly in the value of community and if only I had been meeker when I worked together with others; if only I had trusted more; if only I had turned my gaze upwards more often". And the list goes on and on. These types of statements can paralyse our lives, anchor them in the past and deprive them of power. Biblically speaking, there is no room for "if onlys" because the old has gone; the new is here! (2 Corinthians 5:17), God's mercies are new every morning because great is His faithfulness (Lamentations 3:23), and He will remember no more our sins and transgressions (Hebrews 10:16-17). Life in Christ is a life of second chances for those who, according to the world, are "nobodies" or "useless". By the way, once we recognise that that is what we are, we meet God's requirements!

Given all of this, I consider the book you hold in your hands to be my "second chance", for various reasons. First, because I hope that I have expressed more clearly what I tried to do before. Second, because the intention is also to reflect a reality of the Gospel which I had not yet understood: a gospel that is fuller, freer, deeper, and truer. I want this book to be an offering to God and I hope it is pleasing to Him. And I see it as a gift for you, dear reader, so that it may be a window of hope in your walk with God and in your ministry.

Here, I want to include a sidenote about the profile of the reader I have in mind. Although this book is based on research on the relevance of formal theological education, its aim is to encourage critical reflection on how we carry out education – not only in more formal contexts, but rather, and especially, in the day-to-day contexts of our many ministries and the local church in general. In other words, this book is not exclusively meant to be read by seminary students and theology professors. Rather, it is also meant to be a useful tool in the hands of pastors, workers, and leaders in various ministries. Therefore, when I use the words teacher, professor, or lecturer, I am referring to all those of us who, in one way or another, teach. It may be in the context of the local church or in a specific ministry, in a large or small group, adults or children, in more formal or informal settings. My hope is that any reader who wants to improve their teaching will recognise themselves in this book.

Sidenote ended, I want to recognise that over the years, I have been nourished by the voices of many teachers, through their writings and/or their words, by many colleagues with whom I have had the privilege of working, but above all by the voices of the many people with whom I have had the privilege of serving over the course of many years. You have been my greatest teachers. I hope that the content of this book does you all justice.

The work you are about to read has a small part taken from my doctoral dissertation and another, more extensive part added to make it more comprehensive and relevant. It takes on various risks and it presents a few inconveniences that could potentially weaken my voice. On the one hand, I do not have experience teaching in the context of formal higher education (in fact, I just debuted as a "formal" professor at FIEIDE's Evangelical School of Theology). On the other hand, much of the research I use comes from different geographical and cultural contexts, mainly the American context and to a lesser extent, the British one.

However, I think my contribution is credible and useful for three main reasons. First, as an external observer, I am less influenced by the system and therefore come with fewer pre-conceived notions. Sometimes we need outside voices; sometimes these can even be more influential than internal voices. Second, I come as someone who has received a formal theological education and has worked in ministry for over twenty years. This allows me to point out the shortcomings of formal theological education not only as a witness, but also as someone who understands the field and the needs in the field. Third, I come as an educator and pedagogue, and I contribute this point of view to a field that is basically dominated by theologians. A collaboration between both disciplines is urgently necessary and this combination has the potential of being an important tool in God's hands to renew theological education, which will also affect how His people grow and are truly transformed to extend His kingdom.

# Chapter 1

## The Importance of Theological Formation in Ministry

To learn is to face a transformation. (Palmer 1993, 40)

In May 2017, I carried out a survey[1] among the group of people - mostly pastors and church leaders - attending a Seminar on Theology and Pastoral Psychology, organised by the Spanish Evangelical Alliance. This survey sought to explore three objectives: (1) evaluate the current state of the worker, (2) evaluate the most important needs in terms of support, and (3) evaluate the interest in sabbaticals and times of rest in a specific geographical location.

The objective with the highest score was Objective 2. The results did not take into account whether participants had received training in the past or whether they were receiving it at the time. However, they did show that, to these workers, spiritual formation was not just important to their ministry but that it is the most important training; that they would rather make this investment with the support of others than on their own; that they valued practically all aspects of ministry formation equally (some specified needs regarding formal counselling, language, biblical-theological and pastoral training), and particularly tools such as mentoring and coaching; that training and support are not just important for or limited to a specific moment, rather that they should be something ongoing and an intrinsic part of pastoral ministry. Participants also mentioned mentoring, caring for their relationship with God, and the community of workers for mutual support as the most important resources.

The objective that received the second highest score was Objective 3. Participants mostly agreed that rest is essential to their overall health and that it is important to intentionally withdraw physically. These results seem to align with the overall results of Objective 2: it seems logical that a training that encourages holistic being would also encourage holistic rest. Nevertheless, these results do not necessarily

---

[1] You can request the complete study with the results by writing to me at edithvilamajo@gmail.com.

correlate with reality: although participants understand the importance of rest, they do not make the time for it. It may be that the participants cannot rest due to pressures that are not only ministry related, but that also have to do with family, personal matters, etc. and that these are prioritised, relegating rest to another time. It may be that they do not know how to rest because they follow a leadership model that does not exemplify this area very well: ministry becomes the foundation of the worker's identity, dressed up as sacrificial surrender to the Lord, and rest is equated to laziness, indifference, or lack of commitment. It may be that they do not know how to rest because they do not receive the support they need from their churches/Christian organisations in order to make time for rest and sabbaticals.

Finally, the objective with the lowest score (although it was still a significant amount), was Objective 1. Participants answered the question about the requirements for pastoral/Christian ministry with a good dose of realism: although some of the requirements were well-known, there was also a measure of bewilderment. Perhaps this paradox is the reason workers remain steadfast despite the demands of ministry! Participants seemed to be aware of their own limitations – negative ones, in some cases, such as a lack of confidence or necessary skills to carry out ministry – but on a positive note, they were aware that these limitations enabled them to find the necessary means and resources. As we saw earlier, what the results reflect in terms of training and rest are the best example of this. These results seem to confirm that God will use workers with the gifts He has given them in the circumstances He has put them in, but also through their weaknesses, because God put His "treasure in jars of clay to show that this all-surpassing power is from God and not from us" (2 Corinthians 4:7). In this context, the participants also pointed out the lack of pastoral support from their church/organisation.

Although this survey was carried out at a specific event (so the sample was not objectively randomised), I think that the results are not only valid, but that they also shine a light on the reality of ministry. The people surveyed were aware of their current state and of their needs: continuous holistic training, real support through mentoring and community, as well as a ministry that includes renewing rest. Faced with these results, we cannot remain indifferent, and we must act. They should lead us to ask ourselves seriously: how is theological education responding to these challenges? And how is the church responding?

FOOD FOR THOUGHT

- Do you identify with these results? Why?

## A bird's eye view of the crisis in contemporary theological education

> Learning for religious vocation does not begin by mastering a set of skills or acquiring technical religious formation. It begins by learning to be Christian: truly, deeply, thoughtfully, intelligently, lovingly Christian. This is a wonderfully appropriate curricular goal and a breathtakingly difficult educational task. (Aleshire 2008, 31)

What we will discuss in the following pages, and throughout this book in general, is directly related to institutions of theological education, but it also concerns the Church. I invite you to pay attention because theological education is relevant for both contexts, given that both need each other and should nourish each other: the Church needs theological education and theological education has no reason for being apart from the Church. So, what is the purpose of theological education?

FOOD FOR THOUGHT

- What do you think the purpose of theological education is?

The debate surrounding this is recent, but not new. There is a general discontent that argues that theological education has become irrelevant, clearly lacking purpose and direction, and that it is dry and disconnected from the realities of ministry. Grainger, in his article "The Mission of God as the Focus of Theological Education", sums up some common criticisms of theological education/ministerial formation: a high degree of compartmentalisation in theology and therefore little integration with other disciplines; a disconnect between theory and practice; the professionalisation of theology, which restricts it to an elite group of people rather than all the people of God (Grainger 1994, 69-71). Echoing Grainger, others add the following issues: defining the context (theological education is carried out according to location and history); use of the Bible (which method is the best and correct exegesis); contents (traditional assignments in the curriculum as opposed to specialised assignments that respond to different ministerial needs and how to teach them); the place of mission in the programme; questions of methodology (student centred, teacher centred, assignment or curriculum centred); questions of access (who should have the right to access theological education and what are the admission requirements); modes of education (traditional, academic, or seminary); and theological education as a lifelong process (Aleshire 2008, 49-53; Wingate 2005, 239-244).

These days, we face a landscape with some significant challenges. Institutions of theological education have been greatly influenced by the secular academic world. Even though this has been a positive influence, up to a certain point, the biggest concern is the negative impact. Grainger relates the observations of a group of Third World theological educators regarding British theological institutions: "They wondered whether the strong link with the secular university system was not being maintained at too high a price in sacrificing freedom to determine the content and structure of ministerial formation" (Grainger, 70). Nessan (Nessan 2010, 179-180) and Jaison highlight the pressure to get accredited: "Many theological schools today are little more than technical, degree-granting institutions that often fall under the multiple demands from accrediting bodies on syllabus and academic activities" (Jaison 2015, 2). Witherington adds the problem of an exaggerated focus on the cognitive, explaining that "[...] the church and the academy continue to do theology by and large using an analytical paradigm" (Witherington 2005, 38).

Harkness takes up the general disenchantment from the perspective of students, the Church, and people who serve the Church on a voluntary basis. Students' main concern seems to be that they don't feel sufficiently prepared to deal with the day-to-day realities of ministry (Harkness 2001, 143). The expectation is that seminaries mitigate the problem, and yet they make it worse. Kim describes it as the "crisis of insensitivity of theological education" (Kim 1984, 41). Maybe this is because we are asking the wrong question. Peterson suggests:

> It is not [...] What can we do to make the seminary a better place for spiritual formation? But rather, How can we enter into and embrace the unique condition that constitutes the seminary, in such a way that we grow up into the maturity of Christ Jesus? (Peterson 1997, 57)

Traditional paradigms are no longer relevant for the present-day context and needs. Liefield and Cannell describe the current landscape as a failure of the institution, including faculty and the administration in this (Liefield and Cannell 1992, 249). According to these authors, these last two produce graduates who are ill-equipped to carry out the ministry they have been called to and are incapable of leading, for they have a distorted view of the authority of leadership, an inadequate value of ministry, an insufficient understanding of the purposes of ministry, and a poor integration of exposition and application of the Scriptures (Liefield and Cannell 1991, 21). They highlight the shortcomings of seminary curricula and the obsession with quantity over quality. Collinson agrees and questions "the teaching methods used and the outcomes in the lives and ministry of Theological graduates" (Collinson 2004, 226). Additionally, Kim talks about the failure of institutions to be relevant within the context they have been called to do mission in (Kim 1984, 42).

Other matters aggravate the situation and make this debate even more complex. The student profile has changed, and therefore so has the overall composition of the student body and its needs, but it seems that institutions are not responding to this new reality. Students nowadays do not necessarily want to attend a seminary because of ministerial vocation, but rather for many other reasons, such as getting a degree, deepening their faith and gaining better biblical and theological understanding. Some of them are still very young and do not have a clear idea of what they want to do with their lives. Others haven't even defined their beliefs or their commitment to following Jesus is not very strong. According to Thenelshof, the students of today have "a fragmented identity", a "weak" personal commitment and a lack of spiritual discipline (Thenelshof 2000, 111). We should also take into account the effects of postmodernism, new technologies, the disconnect between theological education and the Church, and the vital need for teachers to show integrity and be examples. Seminaries cannot ignore these undeniable realities. Rather, they must assess these needs and reorganise their priorities.

FOOD FOR THOUGHT

- Do you think that theological education in your country is in crisis? Why?
- Do you think that the institutional theological education in your country responds to the Church's needs?
- How do you think the Church responds to its members and leaders' need for training?

## Voices for the renewal of theological education

Various voices have defended the need to renew theological education.

For James Smith, the key question is: "What if education, including higher education, is it not primarily about the absorption of ideas and information, but about the *formation* of hearts and desires?" (Smith 2009, 18). This author questions the value of an education that is reduced to merely transmitting information, to a cognitive matter, to shaping a specific Christian worldview based on assumptions, or even to beliefs. His proposal is to recapture a more biblical anthropology, which recognises that human beings are more than thinking beings – first and foremost, they are beings that desire, that are passionate, and that feel. Therefore, education must be about "embodied learning", focused on the formation of a "particular people" connected to the mission of the Church.

Robert Banks does not just ask, "What's theological about theological education?", but also, "What's theological about a theological school?"

(Banks 1999, 18). He would agree with Smith, who says that theological education cannot be exclusively academic, but should go a step further by heavily emphasising its practical aspect:

> Orientating the entire theological curriculum to the vocation of the practical theologian overcomes the dichotomy between theory and practice that arose from the attempt to give theology academic respectability through introducing the theological encyclopaedia. (Banks 1999, 36)

He believes that "theological education is a dimension of mission and has a vital missiological content" (Banks 1999, 131) and maintains that its principles emanate from the Bible. He recommends rereading Scripture with this in mind in order to form the basis for renewing theological education today. He does not deny the importance of the academic side and spiritual formation but, he argues, theological education must lead, first and foremost, to practical obedience so that it can be part of what God is doing in the world.

David Kelsey, referring to the same important question, says:

> What distinguishes a theological school is that the subject it seeks to understand truly is *theos*, God [...] Therefore it is more accurate to say that what distinguishes a theological school is that it is a community that studies those matters that are believed to lead to true understanding of God. (Kelsey 1992, 31)

Kelsey presents what have historically been considered the two opposite poles of education. On the one hand, he describes the models of Athens, which centres on forming students so that they grow in wisdom. On the other hand, he describes the Berlin model, more rational and focused on training professionals. Then he proposes a model that lies at the intersection of both paths. His *utopia* for theological education can be summed up as follows:

> A Christian theological school is a community of persons trying to understand God truly by focusing study of various subject matters through the lens of questions about the place and role of those subject matters in diverse Christian worshipping communities or congregations. (Kelsey 1992, 110)

## Redeeming spiritual formation

The crisis in theological education lays bare the disproportionate amount of attention that is put on the academic side of things, to the detriment of spiritual formation. We have institutions with calcified ways and students who arrive at the institution with a passion for God and ministry and leave with a passion for academics. They can do an excellent biblical exegesis, but they are incapable of walking alongside other believers in their moments of pain.

Students should not just know about God. They should also know God. Tenelshof says:

> [Spiritual education] begins with a change from alienation and enmity in relation to God, with which we are all born, into a state of peace and sonship in his family. This change is not complete until the person is fully transformed into the likeness of Christ. To be saved in this life, therefore, means to be in a process of spiritual transformation. (Tenelshof 2000, 112)

It is not enough that students gain information about God, they also need to grow in their relationship with Him. There should not be a single teacher or institution that is satisfied with students who gain knowledge, but not wisdom; that gain information, but whose hearts are not transformed. On the contrary, as Coe suggests, everything we do at a seminary should be a means for students to love God more (Coe 2000, 86). Every time he teaches, Coe asks himself: "Am I encouraging my students in their becoming lovers of God and others, or am I doing 'spiritual violence' to their spirits and faith?" (Coe 2000, 94). At the same time, Liefield and Cannell admit that defining spirituality is practically impossible (Liefield and Cannell 1992, 243) and they suggest that the goal should be to understand it rather than define it.

To be sure, there is a growing intent and willingness to progress when it comes to spiritual formation, but there are, however, also serious gaps that require an answer. We often ask ourselves whether spiritual formation can be taught and, if the answer is affirmative, the question is how can it be taught and how can it be part of the curriculum? Liefield and Cannell note that, when surveyed, the biggest concern for teachers has to do with how to guide others in their spiritual process (Liefield and Cannell, 1992). Often, there is a willingness to include spiritual formation in theological education, but at the same time, there is still a lot of uncertainty about how to do it.

Coe argues forcefully that, although seminaries follow the model of secular universities, which is mostly academic and centres on contents and professional development, spiritual formation should not be consigned to the area of "non-curricular", but rather it should be fully integrated into the curriculum (Coe 2000, 85-86). Additionally, both he and Tenelshof maintain that educators should be intentional when it comes to the process of spiritual formation in students: "The need to be intentional in spiritual formation within Christian education is imperative if we are truly equipping men and women in both mind and character to impact the world for Christ" (Tenelshof 2000, 122). Cheesman addresses the teacher's illiteracy on the topic, challenging them to read "into works that address what it is we are trying to do with our students in the area of spiritual formation" to enrich their teaching (Cheesman 2007, 4). However, Liefield and Cannell point out the fact that spiritual formation cannot be set out in programmes and structures, and they suggest that, although we do use programmes, "what students may need most [...] is the opportunity to witness what God is already doing in their lives and in the lives of others, rather than sitting under still more teaching" (Liefield and Cannell 1992, 248-249). The main objective should be "learning for transformation rather than learning to reinforce received tradition" (Wingate 2005, 242).

Spiritual formation should not and cannot be consigned to second place. However, it should also not be the number one priority, because that would lead us to the same mistake we made with the academic aspect. So, which is the way forward? A growing number of voices are calling for integration. Liefield and Cannell could not be more straightforward when they say that "theology and spiritual formation belong together and inform each other" (Liefield and Cannell 1992, 250).

FOOD FOR THOUGHT

- Do you think that institutes of theological education are responsible for the spiritual formation of their students? Why?
- Do you think that institutions of theological education meet that need? How?
- Do you think the Church concerns itself enough with the spiritual formation of believers? How does it do this?

## The importance of the teaching ministry

For any reader that is not involved in the academic theological environment, these debates may sound completely incomprehensible, since they may not seem to have any connection with the day-to-day work of ministry. However, I believe we may be at a critical crossroads. On the one hand, we have the reality of ministry, which speaks for itself: workers are calling for and need training to carry out their ministries. This demand is either due to the absence of training or due to inadequate training. On the other hand, we have the voices of "experts" who loudly condemn the way in which institutions of theological education have responded to this reality and need. If we proceed on the basis that God's main objective is to transform people to His image, then the Church's teaching ministry is important and necessary. Both the criticisms of the "experts" and the tangible realities in our ministerial daily lives should prompt us to a profound reflection. It should not only prioritise training as part of the agenda for Christian institutions, but also prompt them to do this while searching for the necessary changes that will bring about a fresh take on training. Above all, however, it should be relevant and respond to the daily realities of a worker's ministry. This will result in churches having a growing trust in institutions of theological education and, consequently, more collaboration. In the same way, this will lead to institutions looking for ways to really address the worker's daily ministerial needs.

This is the goal of the book you hold in your hands. Theological education, in both the formal context of seminaries and Bible schools and the informal one of the local church, has the potential to be an awesome tool in the hands of God to bless the Church and the world. And it will fully achieve its purpose when it seeks to not just impart knowledge but also nurture students' souls so that they aim to be more like Jesus and are prepared to be useful in God's hands for his service.

In the first part of this book, chapters 2 to 4, we will focus on the spiritual tools we have at our disposal. In chapter 2, we will present the biblical-theological foundations that back up the idea of a believer's formation as an instrument to transform them into God's image – a redeeming work that God has finished and that, at the same time, is still in progress. In chapter 3, we talk about the role of the Holy Spirit as an agent of transformation: how He acts in people's lives, both teachers' and students', and how we should give Him room to move and fulfil His objectives. In chapter 4, we will study the Word as a tool that invites us into the presence of God and invites us to be part of His great story.

Throughout the second part of this book, chapters 5 to 9, we present various pedagogical tools, and we look at how to read and use them from a biblical perspective. In chapter 5, we will propose an integrated pedagogical approach. In chapter 6, we will address the need to help students be responsible for their own learning process. In chapter 7, we will highlight the importance of learning in community and how to build safe communities for this purpose. In chapter 8, we will talk about how we build ministries that are sustainable in the long term. Finally, in chapter 9, we will focus our attention on caring for teachers, especially their spiritual nourishment, so that they can be prepared for a fruitful teaching ministry. We will wrap up this book with some final thoughts.

# Chapter 2

## Formation for Transformation

> [Spiritual formation] begins with a change from alienation and enmity in relation to God, with which we are all born, into a state of peace and sonship in his family. This change is not complete until the person is fully transformed into the likeness of Christ. To be saved in this life, therefore, means to be in a process of spiritual transformation. (Tenelshof 2000, 112)

Continuing from chapter 1, and as we will reiterate throughout this book, as teachers, we want to invite the people we serve to not only know about God, but to ultimately know God. In other words, we do not want them to merely acquire information about God; instead, we want them to grow in their relationship with Him. We should not be satisfied if people gain knowledge but not wisdom, information but not the transformation of their hearts. We want everything we do to point towards loving God more.

### Food for Thought

"We should not be satisfied if people gain knowledge but not wisdom, information but not the transformation of their hearts. We want everything we do to point towards loving God more."

- Do you agree with this statement? Why?

At first glance, this objective may appear simple, but we should not be surprised or even discouraged if we feel incapable of achieving it. Inevitably, this inability leads us to the question: How? How do we help people to grow spiritually? This question will then lead to others: What is spirituality? Can it be taught? Should we be intentional when it comes to teaching it? How can we measure a person's spiritual growth?

## Food for Thought

- What do these questions suggest to you?
- How would you answer them?
- A good and easy way to start is by helping the people we serve see what God is doing in their own lives and in the lives of others. How can you do this?

When God redeemed humanity through Jesus, His purpose was to make disciples – people who would follow Him committedly and unconditionally. However, becoming a disciple does not happen overnight: it is a lifelong process. The invitation to be more like Jesus involves movement from one state to another state, from the old to the new. When it comes to looking after disciples, the goal should go beyond wanting them to acquire cognitive knowledge of God; it should also, and above all, be for them to know God and to equip them to serve Him. The summons is undoubtedly holistic: the disciple is called to a full transformation. As teachers, we have the immense responsibility and privilege of being in God's hands so that He can use us as agents of transformation.

With this in mind, in this chapter we will first look at how the concept of transformation is understood in the Bible, and we will do so by looking at two specific passages. Second, we will approach the concept of transformation from its theological dimension. This approach, which may seem dry at first, aims to establish firm foundations that will not only enlighten us but also motivate and equip us in our role as agents for transformation in God's hands.

## Transformation from a biblical perspective

The first passage we will consider is Romans 12:1-2, as these verses invite us to explore the biblical idea of transformation:

> Therefore, I urge you, brothers and sisters, in view of God's mercy, to offer your bodies as a living sacrifice, holy and pleasing to God—this is your true and proper worship. Do not conform to the pattern of this world, but be transformed by the renewing of your mind. Then you will be able to test and approve what God's will is—his good, pleasing and perfect will. (Romans 12:1-2)

FOOD FOR THOUGHT

- What do you think this passage says about transformation?
- What characterises the transformation Paul talks about?
- How does it apply to your context?

## No divide between theory and practice

This text first draws our attention to the fact that there is no divide between theory and practice or, in other words, between knowledge and action. The adverb *therefore* may mislead us to think that there is an intentional gap between what Paul has been saying so far in presenting the theory of the truth of the Gospel and what follows, which is clearly more practical. However, nothing is further from the truth. What Paul is now about to say flows from the Gospel presentation he has already expounded.

Paul is not using his own authority, nor does he address the Romans from a purely theoretical standpoint. He speaks as an authorised apostle. His phrase *I urge you* (v. 1), in the imperative mood, could not be more emphatic. He is demanding that the readers respond to the Gospel he has presented earlier in a practical manner. What's more, for Paul, there really is no other way to respond to this request. The people who claim to follow Jesus must act in obedient response to what they have believed as true, so *in view of God's mercies* (v. 1) serves as a reminder of what he has previously declared: the truth of the Gospel.

The word Paul uses to make his plea, *offer* (v. 1), is a sacrificial term that implies that the believer not only responds out of gratitude but that they also give themselves entirely as a gift, repeatedly.

FOOD FOR THOUGHT

- Think about your own Christian life. Can you find specific examples of how you separate theory and practice?

## No divide between mind and body

In this passage, Paul tries to convince and explain that there is no separation between mind and body. In other words, there is no distinction between intellect – the cognitive aspect – and the other parts of the body and a believer's life. God transforms the entire being. The connection between the body (v. 1) and the mind (v. 2) is natural because these verses are not independent, but interdependent. The call, therefore, is to a holistic transformation of both the body and the mind. Furthermore, there is nothing to indicate that the word *body* in verse 1 refers exclusively to the physical body, which makes us think that *your* (sacrifice) refers to all the areas of a believer's life, including their relationships. In other words, it is not just about what the believer can offer God, but about the believer offering him- or herself.

Although the offering of bodies as a living sacrifice is a response to what God has done (v. 1), this should not be taken literally. Paul has chosen to use the figurative sense of sacrificial language to convey the full force of what God requires of every believer. In fact, if taken literally, *living* and *sacrifice* could be interpreted as a contradiction in terms. But it is the paradox created by the combination of two such incongruent terms that is so appealing. On the one hand, Paul's choice to use the word *living* points to the fact that, in literal terms, the animal was brought to the altar alive. In the same way, in figurative language, believers are to present themselves in their newness of life and offer themselves to God.

On the other hand, *living* does not connote a once-and-for-all action, but an ongoing giving of oneself. For believers, offering their bodies as *living sacrifices* becomes *true spiritual worship*. Paul was encouraging his readers to go beyond traditional and public worship; he was urging them to full commitment – not merely as the logical response to the grace of God, but as a rational response that involves both heart and mind in unison.

FOOD FOR THOUGHT

- How could you draw closer to God with your "whole body"?

### No divide between the "now and not yet"

For Paul, transformation is an ongoing process. Although there is not a significant difference between the verbs *to conform* and *to transform*, in this verse they are in contrast because *conform* is used in a negative form and *transform* is affirmative. In the original text, however, both appear in the Greek present passive imperative form, indicating continuity. Once again, this is not something that occurs at a specific time; it is an invitation for believers to a continuous process of transformation that only ends in glorification. Freedom and all the resources found in Christ provide the believer with everything they need to fight against the patterns of this world and to be transformed in every aspect according to His image.

But the question that remains is: How is a believer transformed? Paul declares unequivocally that it is by the renewal of the mind, which, in this context, refers to an individual's ethical and moral judgment. Transformation does not only have to do with what is seen, the external, or with behaviour. It is deep and internal, something that radiates from the inside out, operated by the Spirit of God who lives in everyone who has submitted, and continues to submit, their life to God.

FOOD FOR THOUGHT

- How does "the not yet" invite you to continue towards the goal?
- How can you renew your mind?

## No divide between the responsibility of God and of the believer

Finally, these verses lead us to believe that there is no divide between the role of God and of the believer in the process of transformation. It is a close partnership. The Spirit not only works in believers but also compels them to cooperate with Him. Although it is true that God is the only one who can change hearts, it is also true that the believer, acting of his or her own free will, has the ability to resist or accept His intervention. Gratitude is the most appropriate response to the grace of God, but more than that, the true response is a submissive life that allows His continuous work of transformation to be done, until the believer is formed in Christ.

FOOD FOR THOUGHT

- How do you resist taking your share of the responsibility in your path toward transformation?

The second passage we will study is Colossians 1:24-29. This passage helps us specifically understand what Paul's role was in the transformation of believers and its implications for us as teachers:

> Now I rejoice in what I am suffering for you, and I fill up in my flesh what is still lacking in regard to Christ's afflictions, for the sake of his body, which is the church. I have become its servant by the commission God gave me to present to you the word of God in its fullness— the mystery that has been kept hidden for ages and

> generations, but is now disclosed to the Lord's people. To them God has chosen to make known among the Gentiles the glorious riches of this mystery, which is Christ in you, the hope of glory. He is the one we proclaim, admonishing and teaching everyone with all wisdom, so that we may present everyone fully mature in Christ. To this end I strenuously contend with all the energy Christ so powerfully works in me. (Colossians 1:24-29)

### Food for Thought

- What does this passage say about Paul's role in the transformation of believers?
- What does this imply for you as a teacher?

## Paul's commissioning

As an apostle, Paul was given the responsibility of making known God's plan, revealing the mystery now disclosed. This commissioning must also be understood from an eschatological point of view: the Gentiles are now invited to partake in the Gospel of Christ. Furthermore, Paul is compelled to present the Word of God in its *fullness* (v. 25), where the image here can be understood as an open door to reveal the mystery to the believer: *Christ in you* (v. 27). It is an invitation to an intimate lifelong relationship with Jesus.

Paul is not only called to present the *mystery*, but also to exercise his given authority as an apostle to proclaim Christ *admonishing and teaching everyone* (v. 28). Even though the proclamation of Christ is central, it cannot operate without the other two actions:

> *Teaching and admonishing* are near synonyms, both meaning "instruct." The former carries the implication of exhortation, warning and correction, hence "admonish, warn," and its use in Jewish literature with reference to God chastening. [...] The latter, teaching, more characteristically refers to the skill of the teacher

in imparting practical and theoretical knowledge to the pupil. (Dunn 1996, Electronic Version: Location: 125)

FOOD FOR THOUGHT

- Who gives you the authority to teach?
- How do you use your authority?
- What makes it hard to exert your authority? Why?

## Paul's attitude

The implicit imagery of self-giving, servanthood, sacrifice, model, wisdom, and joy say a lot about Paul's attitude towards his ministry. Not only is he prepared to suffer on behalf of the Colossians, but he also does so joyfully. Paul is well aware that sufferings are part of his apostolic ministry and preaching of the Gospel. However, with these declarations he is not claiming that the sufferings of Jesus were not enough and need to be supplemented by him. The best reading is twofold: he is willing to endure more so that his fellow believers do not have to suffer but there is also an eschatological hint. Suffering is an anticipation of what is to come and, therefore, it is also a reason to rejoice.

His second declaration is that of a servant. He does not use his authority as an apostle for his own purposes. In this passage, Paul is not seeking to attract believers to himself. He is lovingly committed to their welfare and seeks to see them *fully mature in Christ* (v. 28). It is interesting to note the fact that Paul had never visited the church in Colossae personally. Rather, he is following up the work that Epaphras started (Colossians 1:7).

Finally, he carries on his ministry *with all wisdom* (v. 28). He appeals not to his own knowledge and wisdom but to divine wisdom, which stems from his close relationship with God, but also acts as a model to the Colossians for daily living.

FOOD FOR THOUGHT

- As a teacher, how do you cope with your "sufferings"?
- How could you see them as part of your calling, vocation, and training?

## Paul's audience

Paul uses several terms to address the people he is admonishing and teaching: *you* (referring to the Colossians, v. 25, 27), *the Lord's people* (v. 26), *Gentiles* (v. 27), and *everyone* (v. 28). Paul does not intend to admonish and teach only Jews or an elite group of people – he is clearly including Gentiles. This is what the mystery is all about: the Gospel is now available for them as well.

Furthermore, this is for both believers and non-believers alike. *Everyone* is emphatically repeated three times, extending the invitation to all believers, including the Colossians. Paul intends his teaching to apply to all the people he encounters. The Gospel is global.

FOOD FOR THOUGHT

- Think about your Christian life. Are you excluding anyone? Why?
- How could you be more inclusive?

## Paul's goal

Paul's desired goal of admonishing and teaching is to present everyone *fully mature in Christ* (v. 28). This is a term from sacrificial language that means *"to be blameless in character and conduct"*. It is also an eschatological term: the believer's transformational process from one state to the other will finish in glory on the day when believers will have to present themselves before God's throne at the final judgment. The aim of the believer is to experience complete transformation into the image of Jesus.

FOOD FOR THOUGHT

- How would your teaching ministry change if your goal was always "a person's transformation"?

## Paul's resources

It would be a mistake to conclude that Paul does everything purely on his own strength and through his own sufferings and sacrifice, for Paul did have additional resources that helped him faithfully proclaim Christ. Notice how he shifts from the singular *I have become its servant* (v. 25) to the plural form, *we proclaim* (v. 28). Although this could be explained as a simple stylistic choice or even by the fact that Paul had people helping write his letters, it is more likely that Paul is referring to the team that was serving with him (Epaphras in particular) and brought the Gospel to the Colossians.

Paul is indeed committed sacrificially to his ministry, as demonstrated by his efforts *to strenuously contend* (v. 29). The image here is of an athletic contest in which the runner exerts every effort to win the prize. Paul knows his responsibility and responds to it with great effort, yet he is very conscious that it is God who enables him. In other words, it is vital to acknowledge that both humans and God have a responsibility, but work together.

## FOOD FOR THOUGHT

- What resources do you have at your disposal? If you don't have any, why is that?
- Do you make good use of them?

### Relevant points for our ministries

First, both passages address the partnership between God and the believer in the process of transformation. The people we serve cannot change their hearts themselves, but they can position themselves so that God carries out His magnificent work of art in them. In the same way, as teachers, we cannot change the hearts of the people we serve, but we can and should be God's allies in His efforts to do so. God is concerned about the believer as a whole and He offers a deep transformation so they can have a lifetime that will culminate in glory. The work of continual transformation in the believer's life is carried out by the Holy Spirit (a subject we will look at more in depth in chapter 3, "The Holy Spirit as an agent of transformation") and through the renewal of their understanding through the Word (the subject of chapter 4, "The Word that shapes us").

Second, both passages use sacrificial language to denote the giving of oneself and the effort that following Jesus demands. There are obvious implications for the believer and their transformation: it does not come down to merely gaining cognitive knowledge, rather the believer should position themselves before God and allow Him to carry out His work in their life through the formation they receive. It is about submitting one's will, denying oneself. To position oneself implies recognition that one is responsible for one's own process of transformation, instead of living reactively. This is the main theme in chapter 6, "Responsible learning". As teachers, it is very important that we understand what our task is: we should impart knowledge, but we also have to facilitate the process of transformation, making every effort, in partnership with God, so that the people we serve are transformed. We will look at this in more depth in chapter 5, "Integral formation".

Finally, there is an eschatological dimension to both passages that reminds both the people we serve and ourselves as teachers that the transformation we should be looking for is a long-term process, which does not finish at the end of a course. It ends in glory. Our concern should not be, "How can we set up a training programme?", but rather, "How can we equip people to run the race until the end?". This is what we will be looking at in chapter 8 on "A sustainable teaching ministry".

## Food for Thought

- Do you agree with these points? Why?
- Can you think of any others?

## Exercise

- Read the following passages and note what principles you observe regarding the theological concept of transformation:
  2 Corinthians 3:18
  Ephesians 3:14-19
  1 Peter 1:13-23
- Can you think of any other passages? Which ones?

## The theological dimension of transformation

In the day-to-day life of a believer, we can often observe two opposite extremes regarding their own transformation towards maturity in Christ. At one end, are the believers who accept God's work as the primary agent of their transformation, avoiding all personal responsibility. This inevitably leads to an arid plateau – a life that lacks vitality and freshness. On the other end, we find believers who are so focused on their personal responsibility as the primary agent of their transformation that God is relegated from any significant involvement. This inevitably leads to a legalistic effort that thinks that the grace of God is not enough, and these people seek to be transformed through works. These two extremes may explain why we see so little relevant growth in the lives of many believers and, even worse, in the life of God's people as a community. Ultimately, this leads to a tragically inadequate impact in a broken and desperately needy world.

There is no doubt about the importance and the key role the doctrine of sanctification has in the life of the believer. And yet, in the words of Smith: "The vision of transformation, of the mature Christian life, of what it means to be a saint, is a theme that evangelical theologians have not developed well" (Smith 2010, 51). As the Church, we have the opportunity of encouraging formation and transformation in the lives of people, but nevertheless we have succumbed to the influence of modernity and the Enlightenment. We would rather communicate information and appeal to knowledge and reason. We choose what we think gives us a measure of control and security, at the expense of real transformation in people.

### Food for Thought

- Think about the way in which you usually teach people. Is it predominantly based on communicating information? Why?

## A look at the various theologies on sanctification

Sanctification is a common word that describes a believer's journey towards maturity once they have been redeemed. The main theological trends have deliberated and continue to deliberate what responsibility God and human beings have in this process. In the following paragraphs, I want to briefly touch upon each one of these theologies. It will be very concise, and I am aware that it may seem overly simplified and not do them real justice.

First, according to the views of reformed theology, although a believer is invited to strive towards holiness, it is God who is responsible for the process. In addition, it is both a definite act of God and a progressive work of the Spirit in the believer that will only end after death. The purpose is to live a life that is pleasing to God.

Second, and by contrast, the view of Wesleyan theology maintains that the responsibility lies with human beings. Wesley believed that sanctification started at the moment of justification and progressed towards total completion before death. He talked about sanctification or perfection in love. For him, faith in action, or love in action, was key to the process of sanctification.

Last, the Pentecostal view advocates that both God and human beings are responsible. The Holy Spirit has a key role both internally, by indwelling the believer to effect regeneration, and externally, by distributing gifts to equip believers for a life of service that reflects a maturing in sanctification.

It is important that we think about these theologies because they force us to consider the vital question: "Who is responsible for the process of transformation?". By adhering to these thoughts, some would say that the responsibility falls entirely on God; others, on human beings; and still others will propose a combination of both. Without favouring one point of view over another, it is more than reasonable to think that a close partnership is the answer. God is the only one who can change hearts, and yet, as believers, we must cooperate by positioning ourselves for change: "Everyone must be active in the process of their salvation and transformation to Christlikeness" (Willard 2002, 82). We will answer this question in more depth in chapter 3, where we will talk about the role of the Holy Spirit, in chapter 5, where we will discuss teachers and pedagogy, and in chapter 6, where we will focus on the student.

## Conceptual difficulties regarding the theological term *sanctification*

As believers, we generally tend to lean towards either an arid plateau or legalistic effort, as we mentioned previously. The way in which we understand the word *sanctification* can reinforce the tendency towards one extreme or the other. To make matters worse, theological literature on this subject can increase the confusion instead of shedding light on the matter. First, there is tension in how we handle the inherent paradoxes within the concept of sanctification. In line with Paul's words in Romans – "I do not understand what I do. For what I want to do I do not do, but what I hate I do." (Romans 7:15) – we often resolve the tensions between opposing points of view in a very unsatisfactory way. If we consider the history of the Church, a movement will often respond to another by going to the complete opposite extreme. Some examples that illustrate these tensions occur, precisely, in the process of defining the term *sanctification*: grace/free will, faith/works, now/not yet, responsibility/action, Trinity/Holy Spirit, etc. The reality is that it often isn't about "this or that", but rather about "this *and* that". Although it is true that in many cases it is necessary to reconsider and redefine ideas, in most cases the challenge is to learn to live in the paradoxical tension of opposing ideas – even if it is uncomfortable.

Second, there is tension surrounding the etymology of the words that are used to describe the concept of sanctification. We may sometimes think that there are contradictions between the concepts that are used to define *sanctification*, such as the term *total depravity* or the idea that "the image of God is lost or infected". Sometimes we may be led to think that two different words are used to describe the same idea. For example, Horton says, "We show our sanctification, dedication and consecration" (Gundry 1987, 126), even when the difference between these three words is barely noticeable. Sometimes, how an author uses specific words seems to contradict the idea they want to transmit. For example, Hoekema uses the word "try" with regards to the believer's role in their process of sanctification. One is left wondering, "What happens if a believer does not try hard enough?" or, "What happens if a believer does not understand how hard they should try?". Finally, we often come across authors who use an idea and assume that there is a general consensus or a shared understanding of the meaning, even though there isn't. For example, Horton says: "This does not mean that we grow into sanctification, but that we progress in sanctification" (Gundry 1987, 113). What does he mean by "being experts on sanctification", and what does he mean by "progressing in sanctification"? Or when he talks about growing in knowledge: "The Word is important also because along with growth in grace there must be growth in knowledge" (Gundry 1987, 122). What does he mean by "knowledge"? Does he mean cognitive knowledge or the knowledge that leads us to a relationship with God?

Third, we find tension in how we interpret the biblical text. How we understand its purpose will directly influence how we explain it. Although we will expand on this idea in chapter 4, I will share a few notes here. All theologies agree that the Word is God's tool *par excellence* to sanctify a believer. However, it would be a mistake to consider the Word as the only medium of grace. This mistake occurs when the Bible is merely and solely valued as a collection of truths instead of understanding it as the means through which we relate to God and others through the incarnate Truth. In other words, this mistake happens when the Word is seen as a tool that only appeals to the mind instead of to an entire person – body, soul, intellect, affections, and will; when the emphasis is on knowledge and accumulating information rather than on transformation; when the Word is taken as an opportunity for intellectual and abstract theological debates rather than as an invitation to live, experiment, and learn from failures.

Fourth, we find tensions within theology itself. When we consider theological aspects, there are various matters we should take into account. First, a theologian's ideas are interpreted, reinterpreted, and redefined over time. Consequently, understanding and defining a specific theology becomes a complex and difficult task. Second, we also have to take into account the historical development of theological thought – something that has been studied with increasingly more depth over time. Different understandings come to light as the Spirit illuminates in a new way what has already been revealed. For example, from a historical point of view, very little has been written on the Holy Spirit as a teacher (as we will see in chapter 3), and it is only recently that more contributions on this subject have been made. We see another example in the fact that the term *transformation* has only recently been adopted in theological discussions. Finally, "church culture" has contaminated, and continues to do so, the well-meaning definitions of a few specific terms. For example, it is a mistake to use the terms *repentance* and *new repentance* as substitutes for consecration and reconsecration, as it questions the assurance of salvation.

Fifth, we find tensions within ecclesiology, which is quite poor in many traditions. And within most traditional theologies with a seemingly solid ecclesiology, it has become more of an end in itself than a means to an end. The emphasis is on the conversion and the sanctification of the individual for the individual's sake, instead of being of the individual for the community's sake. This brings with it several consequences. On the one hand, a greater emphasis on heaven than on how to live life here and now. On the other hand, faith has become a private matter that no one should interfere with and, therefore, no one is accountable to anyone. Not only does this dilute the ethical emphasis the New Testament puts on sanctification, but it also does not use the healing power of community to its maximum potential (we will delve further into this idea in chapter 7).

All the reasons mentioned so far lead me to suggest that the term *transformation* is a better alternative to describe a believer's journey to maturity.

## Food for Thought

- What is your response to the term *transformation*?
- Do the reasons for using it that were detailed in the previous paragraphs convince you? Why?
- Are there any other reasons you would add?

## The idea of transformation

Peterson says, "If God's purpose in bringing us to himself as a distinct and holy people is to glorify himself in the world [...] To this end, God is concerned to maintain them holy and blameless to the end" (Peterson 1995, 67). Transformation is the process that makes this possible. He adds, "Instead of speaking in terms of progressive sanctification, the New Testament more regularly employs the language of renewal, transformation and growth, to describe what God is doing with us here and now" (Peterson 1995, 136). Transformation suggests more than a change, because change is mainly and exclusively attributed to behaviour. Transformation is also more than training, because training is only the action of another on someone or something. Transformation appeals to the unique work of the Holy Spirit in the life of the believer.

The idea of transformation is preferable because it allows us to contemplate it within the wider context of the doctrine of salvation. Peterson says:

> Sanctification is especially associated with covenant theology and the notion of belonging to God because of the redemptive work of his Son. In its broadest sense, renewal is a more comprehensive term, conveying what is meant by sanctification and glorification, but setting these terms in a creation-recreation framework. (Peterson 1995, 133)

This idea also appeals to the doctrine of creation and recreation (glorification in eschatological terms), based on the idea that human beings were created in the image of God, *imago Dei.* Hoekema says that the fact that human beings have been created in God's image "sets man apart from the rest of God's creation, by indicating that he was formed in a unique way [...] He was to mirror God [...] and also represents God" (Hoekema 1986, 66).

Later, through a wilful act of foolishness, human beings are marred by sin. The image of God is not destroyed, but it is broken, ruined; it ends up removed from its original state. Consequently, sin affects human beings' relationship with God, with themselves, with others, and their relationship with all of creation.

However, through God's act of amazing grace, it is possible for His children to search for a new humanity and a new creation when they step out on the adventure of being transformed from glory to glory. A creation-recreation approach reflects Smith's suggestion for a new anthropology in which:

> Human persons are understood not as fundamentally thinking machines but rather as believing animals, or essentially religious creatures, defined by a worldview that is pre-rational or supra-rational. What defines us is not what we think – not the set of ideas we assent to – but rather what we believe, the commitments and trusts that orient our being-in-the-world. (Smith 2009, 43)

## Conclusion

Transformation is God's plan to restore humanity back to its original *imago Dei*. It operates within the context of a relationship with God and union in Christ. Transformation points to the new creation where all things will be made new. All believers will be glorified as their *imago Dei* is restored. This chapter sets out the reasons for why we talk about the need for formation for transformation. The following chapters will establish the resources for this – both spiritual and pedagogical – which will help us underpin the type of formation that leads to transformation.

# Chapter 3

## The Holy Spirit as an Agent of Transformation

> Anointed teaching is first and foremost the result of the presence and power of the Holy Spirit. (Wilhoit and Rozema 2005, 251)

When I was little, I used to say: "When I grow up, I want to go to Africa, build a school and teach". I have never lost sight of that vocation. But before I could become a teacher, I first needed to be a student. I was never actually a brilliant student, however, I kept going because I was willing, I was disciplined, and I worked hard. As I mentioned in the introduction, I know my progress was better when the teachers were friendly, helpful, and encouraging; when they taught their subjects passionately and I could see the link between their teachings and real life. Interactive activities and opportunities to take initiative not only helped me learn, but also helped me flourish as a person.

At the university, during my studies in pedagogy, I was persuaded that the world could be changed through education. This undoubtedly shows how naïve and immature I was at the time, as well as how ignorant I was of biblical reality! However, I don't think they actually taught me how to teach, so when I started teaching, I taught the same way I had been taught. My earliest memory is in the context of my first season of ministry, as a staff worker with the Spanish student movement GBU.[1] At a camp, I taught a seminar to a group of Christian university students titled: "How to develop a Christian mindset". I talked non-stop for ninety minutes and, although I was probably out of breath by the end, I was quite pleased with myself. After all, I had painstakingly prepared the content. After some time, the students had the guts to tell me how boring that session had been. I doubt they learned much!

It may be that this incident is what kindled an ardent desire to search for better ways to teach, so that the students would actually learn. In other words, how could I teach in such a way that students would not only fill their minds with information, but also see their lives transformed? I

---

[1] GBU (Grupos Bíblicos Unidos) is associated with the International Fellowship of Evangelical Students.

found some satisfaction when I started delving into methodological aspects and into the idea that how one teaches can help or hinder the learning process. As an educator, I still believed in the power of education! However, more recently, something even more powerful and true has not only surprised me, but also captivated me. It was undoubtedly the missing piece of the puzzle.

God's desire is to see His children transformed into His image. As teachers, this should also be our greatest desire and, at the same time, our greatest undertaking. We must do everything within our power to steer people towards Christ so that they may be transformed. For this reason, the task of teaching holds a central role in the Church. Before He died, Jesus clearly instructed His disciples to go and make more disciples. And this task included teaching them to obey everything He had commanded them (Matthew 28:20). However, the responsibility of that labour bearing fruit would not fall on their shoulders, nor would it be the responsibility of future followers of Jesus. It would depend on the One who, being appointed by God, would take over this task: "But the Advocate, the Holy Spirit, whom the Father will send in my name, will teach you all things and will remind you of everything I have said to you" (John 14:26). Today, not only is the Holy Spirit the ultimate Teacher, but He is also the transforming agent in the lives of people on their pilgrimage towards glory. Understanding this was a turning point in my own learning process.

In light of the numerous and repeated biblical exhortations about the role of the Holy Spirit as a teacher and His work in our lives, it almost seems ridiculous to have to ask the question: What does the Holy Spirit have to do with teaching? Or an even more obvious question is: What is the role of the Holy Spirit in the process of transformation of a Christian student?

## Food for Thought

- Have you ever asked yourself these questions?
- What are your answers? Why?

However, this question becomes necessary, and I would even say urgent, precisely because it has often been overlooked. Biblical, theological, and pedagogical reflection on the role of the Holy Spirit in education has been conspicuously absent and it is only in the last few years that this subject has started to be talked about in the context of education.[2] This is especially shocking if we take into account that mainstream theologies agree that, out of the three persons of the Trinity, the Holy Spirit is primarily responsible for transformation in the life of a believer. That is also the reason why we teach: we want to see lives transformed!

What could the reasons behind this omission be? It may have been for reasons related to denomination. At the end of the day, there is no consensus on what the role of the Holy Spirit is – whether He operates in submission to the rest of the Trinity or whether He has His own identity and responsibility; whether He has more or less power; whether He has eternal validity or whether He is limited by time and space. Another reason may be the perpetual debate about who is responsible in the process of transformation, as we discussed in chapter 2. Does the responsibility lie with the person who wants to change? Does it lie with the teacher? Does it lie with the Holy Spirit? All these reasons, and many others, have only managed to distract us. And so, I ask myself: Is it not precisely this omission that is causing us to not see better, more visible, and more satisfactory results in our teaching? We often justify ourselves by saying that these results are due to students who lack commitment, interest, discipline, and motivation; to inadequate or irrelevant curricula, and to the lack of resources in general; to the absence of support when it comes to training, moral, emotional, and spiritual matters. But we should also ask ourselves whether the reason our teaching does not bear fruit is because it lacks power – the power of the Holy Spirit, who is the ultimate agent of transformation, working in and through us in the lives of those we minister to.

---

[2] A recently published book that captures a comprehensive look at the role of the Holy Spirit in teaching is Robert Pazmiño and Octavio Esqueda's *Anointed Teaching: Partnership with the Holy Spirit*, 2019, Publicaciones Kerigma.

### Food for Thought

- Do you resist the Holy Spirit?
- If you answered affirmatively, what are your main reasons for this? Why?

Teachers are not the main agents of transformation in a student's life, the Holy Spirit is: "What the Spirit is doing in other persons far exceeds what we ourselves are doing" (Peterson 1994, 186). Nevertheless, He invites us to partner with Him, and that is what makes the power multiply! What an immense privilege! May this truth be a turning point in our pilgrimage as teachers.

### Food for Thought

- How does the Spirit manifest Himself throughout your life and in your day-to-day?
- How does He manifest Himself in you as a teacher?
- By contrast, how does the flesh manifest itself?

## Living in the Spirit

Our starting point should be that the Christian teacher is a new creation in Christ: "The work of God's Spirit in the lives of regenerate teachers is needed so that they may be effective instruments in the hands of God" (Zuck 1998, 6). This means that the Holy Spirit has already exercised in us His role of convincing us of our sin:

> When he comes, he will prove the world to be in the wrong about sin and righteousness and judgment: about sin, because people do not believe in me; about righteousness, because I am going to the Father, where you can see me no longer; and about judgment, because the prince of this world now stands condemned. (John 16:8-11)

Therefore, even if it seems obvious, we cannot expect the Holy Spirit to empower us as teachers if He is not part of our lives. Consequently, those of us who have the Spirit of God in us are called to live in the Spirit, and this implies submitting to Him and allowing His ongoing work in our life. This kind of life will bring us peace (Romans 8:6).

If we want to teach with power, we must first be taught be the One who *is* the power to change us and transform us into the image of God, for "[s]piritual maturity is not something to be achieved by human effort, but received through the transformation work of the Holy Spirit" (Wardle 2004, 18). Because, when we live in the Spirit and our primary objective is to see lives transformed, we leave behind personal interests and ambitions, the need to enforce a curriculum or a plan, power struggles, the desire for promotions, and rivalries between colleagues and authorities. These desires are a reflection of living in the flesh instead of living in the Spirit. We tend to worry and concentrate on doing rather than being. We should remember that, as Christian teachers, our main motivation should not be to prove our knowledge, abilities, wisdom, importance, etc., but rather to guide people towards Christ so they allow the Holy Spirit to work in their lives to reach maturity in Christ. Indeed, we feed and maintain this motivation when we make sure that we do not just say we follow Christ, but when we do everything necessary to walk with Him every day. And this inevitably implies renouncing oneself and submitting to Him. Our transformation bears fruit when it goes well beyond a change in attitude, and when a permanent change of character becomes evident.

As teachers, we must firmly base our identity on who we are in Christ. When we stop to think about Jesus and His ministry, we see that He receives the

Holy Spirit's blessing and the Father's acceptance before He starts His ministry. In the same way, we must remember and treasure that God does not accept us because of what we do but because of who we are. An identity that is anchored in who we are in Christ helps prevent the appearance of motivations that clash with God's true purposes. This secure identity helps us be aware that we (and not just our students) are on a pilgrimage of transformation. This puts us in the position of students, with the same subsequent limitations, weaknesses, and needs. And our humble attitude of dependence on Someone who is not only external to us but also greater than us, creates a model students can identify with and that they can also imitate. This reliant attitude frees us to encourage our students to seek this same subjection for themselves; it makes it possible for students to not look to us – which, after all, will only inflate our egos and distract us from putting our safety in Christ – but to seek the Holy Spirit, who is the one who will truly transform their lives. With our help, our students learn to become aware of the presence of the Holy Spirit and, consequently, we help them to respond in obedience to His movement.

## Additional Resources

**Becoming aware of the presence of the Holy Spirit**

The day-to-day rhythm of our modern-day society barely allows time for silence and listening. How do we position ourselves to give the Holy Spirit space? Wardle proposes four key elements (Wardle 2004, 52):

1. Look for a sacred space to meet with God in.
2. Set aside enough time for it, without rushing.
3. Become attentive to the presence of God.
4. Practise spiritual disciplines to help position yourself in the presence of God.

When we accept our calling, gifts, and responsibilities, and we submit to the Holy Spirit, we become His best partners. "Human teachers should seek to be under the full control of the Spirit, as clean and capable instruments" (Zuck 1998, 72).

## Receiving power from the Holy Spirit

The Spirit calls and gives power. "The wind blows wherever it pleases. You hear its sound, but you cannot tell where it comes from or where it is going. So it is with everyone born of the Spirit." (John 3:8). We will never know exactly how the Holy Spirit moves, but we do know that He moves! Anyone who submits to God receives the Holy Spirit and, in this context of a committed life, as we saw in chapter 2 – living sacrifice (Romans 12:1), a non-conforming life (Romans 12:2), a life worthy of the calling we have received (Ephesians 4:1) – we also receive the gifts of the Spirit (1 Corinthians 12:7).

These gifts, which are distributed according to His grace (Romans 12:6; 1 Corinthians 12:11, 18; Ephesians 4:11), are received gifts, special manifestations of the Spirit (1 Corinthians 12:7), which we are to use to bless others (1 Corinthians 12:7; Ephesians 4:12), as service to the body of Christ, which is the Church, in order to favour its growth towards maturity. We are exhorted to live as one body (Romans 12:4; 1 Corinthians 12:14; 20, 27), without thinking of ourselves more highly than we ought (Romans 12:3), and, therefore, gifts should not be considered for each person's own use, without being consecrated for the use of others in humility and generosity. We have different gifts, but we are one body (Romans 12:4), so these gifts should not be a reason for division in the body, nor a reason to belittle or reject others, since we are all necessary and all the members of the body need each other (1 Corinthians 12:21).

### FOOD FOR THOUGHT

- What gifts do you have?
- How do you know what your gifts are?
- How are you using them?

- Do you have the gift of teaching?
- How do you know?
- How does God reveal Himself in your teaching?

Although it is true that the Bible exhorts us all to teach (for example in Matthew 28:19-20), it is also true that the Spirit specifically distributes the gift of teaching (Romans 12:7; 1 Corinthians 12:28; Ephesians 4:11). This suggests that, although all of us can (and should!) teach, due to both the biblical mandate and natural ability, some, chosen by God, will have a special gift. "A Christian teacher with the gift of teaching does not necessarily know the Bible better than others, but the gift does enable him to impart more effectively what he does know" (Zuck 1998, 61).

When they teach, the primary responsibility of teachers is to equip the body of Christ so that believers in turn can exercise their gifts for the benefit of others:

> So Christ himself gave the apostles, the prophets, the evangelists, the pastors and teachers, to equip his people for works of service, so that the body of Christ may be built up until we all reach unity in the faith and in the knowledge of the Son of God. (Ephesians 4:11-13a)

The Church does not work with the gifts of only a few. Rather, it needs the gifts of many. Our responsibility, through our gift of teaching, is to multiply – a subject we will study in more depth in chapter 8: "And the things you have heard me say in the presence of many witnesses entrust to reliable people who will also be qualified to teach others" (2 Timothy 2:2). Perhaps that is why the gift of teaching is third in the passage in 1 Corinthians. The fact that Paul highlights this gift as an important gift does not detract from the other gifts because, as we have seen, all of them are necessary. Nevertheless, the apostle does highlight the fact that this gift is key to mobilising believers. Consequently, as teachers, we cannot underestimate our responsibility; indeed, we should take it very seriously. Additionally, this text makes us see clearly that our gift is to be used, in partnership with the Holy Spirit, to lead everyone to perfect maturity in Christ, and going back to the true purpose of teaching: "The Holy Spirit does not replace Christian teachers. He chooses to teach through us and throughout ministry to others, as we rely on His power to accomplish His purpose in building the Lord's Church" (Esqueda 2008, 85).

If Christian education and the Christian teacher aim for people's transformation, "[t]he Spirit's work in education makes it a divine, supernatural ministry" (Zuck 1998, 157). This is the main reason why a teacher should not just pursue the exercise of excellent teaching but should also pursue anointed teaching. Wilhoit and Rozema define it as follows:

> The Holy Spirit coming upon the teacher in a special manner. It is God giving insight, power, and enabling through the Spirit to the teacher in order that he/she may do this work in a manner that lifts it up beyond simple human efforts and endeavours. (Wilhoit and Rozema 2005, 240)

Just like a flame, our gift runs the risk of dying out if we do not stoke the fire. For this reason, it is also our responsibility to take care of the gift we have been granted by the Spirit, as Paul urges Timothy to do: "For this reason I remind you to fan into flame the gift of God, which is in you through the laying on of my hands" (2 Timothy 1:6). How do we fan the flame of our gift?

## Food for Thought

- How do you fan into flames your gift/gifts?

First, the Word not only encourages us to desire spiritual gifts, but it says we should do so eagerly (1 Corinthians 14:1; see also 12:31). Desiring these gifts with the right motivation and the proper purpose in mind is admirable. Second, we should remember that God distributes gifts so that they are used (Romans 12:6), and to do so according to God's purposes. A failure to do so puts our own spiritual health and the spiritual health of the Church in general in danger and it grieves the Spirit (Ephesians 4:30). Third, God is the one who trains us, and we must trust in that - not in our own strengths. In this line, Paul says to Timothy: "For the Spirit God gave us does not make us timid, but gives us power, love and self-discipline" (2 Timothy 1:7). However, as we have already mentioned, this all goes hand in hand with living a life that reflects our calling: "Anointing is not merely detected in the passion of the speaker or in an insightful application of the text, but in the very fabric of the message and in the seamless integrity between the life of the speaker and the message" (Wilhoit and Rozema 2005, 239).

## Cooperating with the Holy Spirit

### FOOD FOR THOUGHT

- What are some of the Holy Spirit's names that are related to the role of teacher and His transforming power in people's lives?
- What are some of His purposes as a teacher?

As we have repeated several times, the Holy Spirit is the greatest agent in the process of transformation of a Christian student. In chapter 2, we gave a very broad overview of its theological dimension. I believe it is worth mentioning a few more points here that are related to the educational context.

For the Holy Spirit, exerting His transforming power in people's lives is inherent to both His nature and His purposes.

## Additional Resources[3]

**Names of the Holy Spirit related to teaching**

- Spirit of wisdom and understanding
- Spirit of counsel and power
- Spirit of knowledge and fear of the Lord
- Spirit of truth
- Counsellor
- Spirit of wisdom and revelation

## Additional Resources[4]

**The Holy Spirit's teaching ministries**

- Instructs
- Reminds
- Guides
- Declares
- Reveals
- Inspires
- Convinces
- Dwells
- Enlightens

---

[3] Taken from Zuck, Roy B. (1998). *Spirit-Filled Teaching. The Power of the Holy Spirit in Your Ministry.* Nashville, TN: World Publishing. Chapter 2.
[4] Taken from Zuck, Roy B. (1998). *Spirit-Filled Teaching. The Power of the Holy Spirit in Your Ministry.* Nashville, TN: World Publishing. Chapters 3 and 4.

Reducing theological teaching and learning to just transmitting information could be considered spiritual suicide. The truths of the Bible are to produce transformation: "Spiritual depth is measured not by the extent of one's knowledge of the Scriptures but by the consistency of one's "walk" (conduct) in accord with God's standards" (Zuck 1998, 113). What's more, trying to comprehend transformation through the human intellect is simply impossible (Erickson 1983, 795). It is something that goes beyond what we, as humans, can control and do.

When both student and teacher have an open and obedient attitude to the work of the Holy Spirit, He can move freely in any teaching and learning context, and in many different ways, so that the way in which this transformation operates is very varied:

> As a Teacher, He makes others wise; gives understanding, counsel, power, knowledge, and the fear of the Lord; communicates and applies God's truth; helps in every learning situation; provides spiritual wisdom; and discloses knowledge regarding God. (Zuck 1998, 18)

The Spirit does not just work in us as teachers, rather we must also accommodate His work in all aspects of the educational process: preparation, methodology, and methods, etc. Often it is not just culture that influences us, but also our own comfort - they shackle us in such a way that there is no room for the Holy Spirit to move. Preparing, organising, creating methods, and trying methodologies are not necessarily incompatible with the Spirit's movement but they can quickly become barriers if these are done with an attitude of control and pre-eminence. All these practices must be tools that always serve our purpose of seeing lives transformed. But at the same time, we are called to live in the present moment to be aware of the Spirit's movement, to be fully in fellowship and partnership with Him.

## Additional Resources

**Living in the present moment**

Our problem is not that the Lord is not present, rather that we are not aware of this intimate and transforming presence. Since we focus our attention so much on past/future worries, we are closed off to the realities of the present moment. We have eyes that do not see and ears that do not hear. We are not attentive to what is happening; we are preoccupied with anxious concern, seduced away from the present moment (Wardle 2015, 9).

Jesus was aware of our innate struggle with our day-to-day concerns because He said: "Therefore I tell you, do not worry about your life, what you will eat or drink; or about your body, what you will wear. Is not life more than food, and the body more than clothes?" (Matthew 6:25). However, His invitation is to live in the present moment. This attitude also leads us to pray without ceasing – that is, to be aware of the presence of the Lord in our lives and the fact that we can always draw near to Him.

Therefore, this implies that we must be prepared and open to change course if necessary. We are called to facilitate the movement of the Spirit in students' lives and not to be stumbling blocks.

## Food for Thought

- If you were to test the temperature of your "spirituality", what would you find?
- What is your plan of action to raise the temperature?
- How would living more fully in the Spirit bring more power to your teaching?

## Conclusion

The biblical teachings regarding gifts always go hand in hand with love (Romans 12:9; Ephesians 4:16), which, in the end, should be the mark that sets apart every authentic Christian community: the community of learning (a subject we will dive into in chapter 7). Paul brilliantly sets out this idea in these well-known verses:

> If I speak in the tongues of men or of angels, *but do not have love*, I am only a resounding gong or a clanging cymbal. If I have the gift of prophecy and can fathom all mysteries and all knowledge, and if I have a faith that can move mountains, *but do not have love*, I am nothing. If I give all I possess to the poor and give over my body to hardship that I may boast, *but do not have love*, I gain nothing. (1 Corinthians 13:1-3, emphasis added)

Clearly, he elevates the role of love over everything else, and as Wilhoit and Rozema say: "In one word, the fruit of anointed teaching is love!" (Wilhoit and Rozema 2005, 253). The challenge is the same as the one we raised at the beginning of the chapter – we need to test what our true motivations are when we teach and adjust them, so that our lives are truly a reflection of the life we have been called to: a life in the Spirit.

Having said this, it is interesting to recall what Peterson says: "We are formed by the Holy Spirit in accordance with the text of Holy Scripture. God does not put us in charge of forming our personal spiritualities. We grow in accordance with the revealed Word implanted in us by the Spirit" (Peterson 2011, 29). Giving priority to the Holy Spirit cannot cancel out the priority of the Word, nor vice versa. Both are essential and must feed each other. That is why we will now move on to exploring the role of the Word in our teaching, enlightened by the work of the Spirit in our lives.

# Chapter 4

## The Word that Shapes Us

> Shall we try to control the Bible, that is, try to make it "come out right", or shall we simply seek to release its life into our lives and into our world? Shall we try to "tilt" it this way or that, or shall we give it complete freedom to "tilt" us as it will? (Foster 2010, 6)

Some time ago, someone suggested to me that I might already have enough biblical head knowledge. She then challenged me to start a "downward" journey rather than continuing to deepen, broaden, and collect more information. My first reaction to these words was annoyance. But, as I allowed these words to speak to me, I understood that maybe it was time to deepen the knowledge I had acquired. It was time to give greater importance to the need for the Word to penetrate and lead me to real transformation, to make mine what I already knew, to allow the Word to chip away at me, and open the door to a living and fresh encounter with the Lord of the Word. Interestingly enough, this happened around the time when I was experiencing a feeling of intense overload and my thirst would drive me to meditate on short portions of the Bible, instead of spending long periods of time reading and painstakingly studying it. My very being was telling me to pause and contemplate.

Consequently, this also led me to consider various matters that were not just related to my own experience of reading the Bible, but also the way in which I had used it in my ministry – a way that was strongly influenced by how others had used the Bible to teach me. I started to wonder: What would happen if the Word was simply an invitation to meet with God so that I could be transformed? The paradigm shift I propose in this chapter is that reading the Word should not lead exclusively to an exegesis of the text, but rather to an exegesis of the heart. In my ministry, I want to see the people I serve as more than people who know the Word; I want to see them as people who are deeply changed by the God of the Word.

FOOD FOR THOUGHT

- In one word, how would you describe your relationship with the Word?

## The Word as an invitation to meet with God

The Word of God invites us to position ourselves so that we meet the living God. Ultimately, what we want to see – or what we should want to see – is how we turn into real lovers and followers of Jesus. We want to see our hearts changed for the glory of our Saviour and Lord. We want to set out on a process – a journey of spiritual formation that will only end when Jesus calls us to our eternal home. Therefore, the invitation is for our involvement to go beyond the cognitive: it implicates our entire being and it invites us to discern what the Spirit wants to do.

Time and again, we need to remind ourselves that the Word is *the Word*: "In the beginning was the Word, and the Word was with God, and the Word was God" (John 1:1). We have the chance to position ourselves before the Word in order to encounter the God of the Word, the only one who is worthy of worship and praise. The creed calls on the Trinity – God the Father, Jesus Christ, and the Holy Spirit – and not on the trio of "God the Father, Jesus Christ, and the Holy Bible", which would be a misplaced sacramentalisation of the Bible. It is essential that the people we serve understand that the Bible is not just a source of orthodox doctrine but also, and especially, a source of spiritual sustenance: "the way in which we nurture our soul".[1] The Word should not just be understood as a set of rules to be followed but also, and especially, as a tool to encounter God and be transformed by Him. Scripture introduces us to a God that has spoken and who deserves to be worshipped. The Bible, therefore, is neither a magic wand nor an object of our adoration. The Bible should be believed, and the focus should be on respectfully interpreting the text and faithfully obeying it, not on endless

[1] This idea is taken from Bacote, Miguélez and Okholm 2004, 11.

discussions and arguments about aspects that, at the end of the day, are secondary.

When we train people so that they know Scripture, we must instil in them convictions and attitudes towards it, and talk about the privilege that it is to delight in it and in its benefits and power.

## Additional Resources

**Basic beliefs about the Bible**

- The Bible is the Word of God.
- The Bible can be adequately understood through the translations we have.
- The Bible is a unit. The OT and the NT are complimentary: the OT prepares the way for the NT and the NT fulfils the OT.
- The Bible is its own interpreter – one passage sheds light on another.
- Biblical language is mostly normal human language.
- Our understanding of the Bible should be accompanied by an honest, intelligent, and obedient response to its message (2 Timothy 3:17).
- The Holy Spirit's teaching ministry is necessary in order to understand the Bible (John 16:13; 1 Corinthians 2:14).
- The Word has something to say to me.
- The Word is alive – it always has something new to say to me.

**Attitudes of the heart towards the Bible**

- A humble heart (1 Corinthians 8:2)
- A heart full of faith (1 Peter 1:13)
- A new heart (1 Corinthians 2:14)
- A hungry heart (1 Peter 2:2)
- An obedient heart (Psalm 119:98-100)

- A disciplined heart (Matthew 7:7)
- A teachable heart (Isaiah 50:4)

- Can you think of any other beliefs and attitudes regarding the Bible? What are they?

When we settle for discipleship programmes we can control, we run the risk of no longer concerning ourselves with guiding people to an encounter with Jesus. We must be careful to not fall for the hidden assumption that if we communicate knowledge – intellectual knowledge, that is – then people will be able to apply the Word to their life themselves. Sadly, this is often not true, and what's worse is that often people don't even want to change. Applying the text to our lives should not be a "P.S." at the end of a letter – something that summarises an objective truth instead of leading people towards real changes and concrete actions. It should also not be a footnote – an integral part of the body of the text, but still separate enough that the reader has the option to read it or not. That would be even worse!

The Christian life is an invitation to engage as followers of Christ, not to remain spectators. We long for believers to want to draw nearer to the Word because they know that that is where they will find their God: the God who invites them to step in and be part of His story.

## Building bridges towards understanding Scripture

In the previous chapter, we took a comprehensive look at the role of the Holy Spirit in our teaching ministry. We do not know exactly how the Holy Spirit moves, but we do know He blows where He wills (John 3:8). Nor can we manipulate Him to act in a certain way in our lives, according to what is convenient for us. What we do know is that Jesus promised that the Counsellor, the Holy Spirit, would teach us everything and would remind us of everything Jesus said (John 14:26). When we position ourselves before the Word, we are giving it permission to touch us and act when and how He wants, so that we are transformed. Therefore, the Spirit is our greatest and best tool to build bridges that will help both us and the people we serve in our understanding of the Word.

When we draw near to Scripture with the aim of being trained, both as teachers and as disciples, then we are at the same level, humbly positioned before the One who trains us. Our intention, therefore, is to expose our hearts in a sincere way so that Scripture, which is inspired by God, teaches us, convicts us, and instructs us (2 Timothy 3:16). As teachers, this humble attitude of being touched and transformed strips us of the pretence of being experts in biblical texts, of being responsible for the transformation of the people we serve, or of attributing their successes and progress to ourselves. On the contrary, the door is wide open for us to level the playing field and help the people we serve to not see the Word as a threat, but as a warm and accessible invitation to the Scriptures. Even though there may not be much knowledge and reading of the Bible, we don't see that reality as a barrier, but rather as an opportunity to help people become passionate about the God of the Word, the One who is not just capable of transforming their lives but who also desires to do so. We must make sure that we provide a safe place for people to build up their trust so that they draw near and experience this vital encounter.

The experience of drawing close to the Word in order for it to train us calls on us to involve our whole being. That said, it is necessary to introduce different ways of reading the Bible – ways that go beyond using the mind, beyond a purely cognitive reading, beyond a desire to accumulate more and more information, beyond a distorted emphasis on rational and empirical truth in the process of understanding the text. When we engage our whole being, it allows our understanding of biblical truths to be fresh instead of dry, and it helps us maintain an emotional connexion with the text. And, at the same time, this protects us from the danger of separating heart and mind.

When we prompt the use of emotions, when we appeal to people's willingness, when we give room to our imagination, when we invite people to feel the text with all their senses – smell it, hear it, touch it, taste it – we open the door to reaching new depths.

## Additional Resources

**Verses that speak to the whole body**

*Psalm 34:8*
Taste and see that the Lord is good; blessed is the one who takes refuge in him.

*1 John 1:1-4*
That which was from the beginning, which we have heard, which we have seen with our eyes, which we have looked at and our hands have touched—this we proclaim concerning the Word of life. The life appeared; we have seen it and testify to it, and we proclaim to you the eternal life, which was with the Father and has appeared to us. We proclaim to you what we have seen and heard, so that you also may have fellowship with us. And our fellowship is with the Father and with his Son, Jesus Christ. We write this to make our joy complete.

*Matthew 11:15*
Whoever has ears, let them hear.

*Romans 10:17*
Consequently, faith comes from hearing the message, and the message is heard through the word about Christ.

*Psalm 119:103*
How sweet are your words to my taste, sweeter than honey to my mouth!

*Matthew 26:26-29*
While they were eating, Jesus took bread, and when he had given thanks, he broke it and gave it to his disciples, saying, "Take and eat; this is my body." Then he took a cup, and when he had given thanks, he gave it to them, saying, "Drink from it, all of you. This is my blood of the covenant, which is poured out for many for the forgiveness of sins. I tell you, I will not drink from this fruit of the vine from now on until that day when I drink it new with you in my Father's kingdom."

> *1 Peter 2:3*
> [...] now that you have tasted that the Lord is good.
>
> *Matthew 5:6*
> Blessed are those who hunger and thirst for righteousness, for they will be filled.

When our love for the God of the Word grows, and it is a real and authentic love, then our thirst to increase our intellectual knowledge of Scripture will also grow because we know, through experience, that this knowledge is not hollow. By definition, it leads us to greater intimacy with the God of the Word. Therefore, our main challenge lies in developing our ability to listen, recognise the voice of God, and practise an attitude of obedience in order to fulfil the Scriptures in our lives. It does not lie in the often uncontrollable need to debate a text in order to understand it.

## Additional Resources

**Historical-grammatical method of interpretation**

This is the method that has been most widely used and, although it has its strong points – such as taking into account the genre of the text, the historical context, and the author's intended meaning – strictly historical methods have come under increasing criticism because they divorce historical study from theology, don't require obedience or praxis, don't necessarily lead to transformation, ignore the ecclesial context of Scripture (in particular the reception of Scripture), and distort the nature of the Bible itself (Colijn, 2004). Some other reasons:

- The focus on discovering what the author wants to say can often lead to a poor connexion with what God may want to say today. This can lead to thinking that the text is not relevant for our daily context.
- The focus on rational and empirical truth in the process of understanding the text can often lead to only using the mind instead of the whole body. This results in a dry understanding of the truths of Scripture and an emotional disconnect. It produces a serious decoupling of heart and mind.

- The focus on information tends to prioritise intellectual knowledge over heart knowledge and putting the truths of Scripture into practice.
- Do you agree with this position? Why?

We want to connect the text with what God can say today, and not just discover what the original author meant to say. This presents us with the opportunity to see the relevance of the text for our own context and, ultimately, for our own life. Drawing near to the text and allowing it to shape us and leaving room for heart knowledge paves the way for sound doctrine as well as for a healthy practice of the truths of Scripture.

## Additional Resources

Introducing different ways of reading Scripture can significantly enrich our experience:

**1. Devotional method**

The devotional method entails choosing a passage and, through prayer and meditation, allowing the Holy Spirit to show us the path to applying His truth in our life in a personal, practical, possible, and measurable way.

a. Pray that you will know how to apply the passage.

b. Meditate (ponder) on the passage:

- Visualise (imagine) the scene,
- Stress words from the key verse,
- Paraphrase (make it your own).

c. Ask yourself the following questions:

· Is there a sin I should confess?

· Is there a promise I can claim for myself?

· Is there a commandment I should obey?

· Is there an example to follow?

· Is there a mistake to avoid?

· Is there a truth to believe?

· Is there something to praise God for?

· What does this passage teach me about Jesus/God/humans/myself?

d. Write down how it applies to you personally.

It must be personal and start with "I"; it must be practical and be expressed with an action verb; it must be possible, something achievable; it must be something measurable, that can be evaluated.

e. Memorise the key verse.

**2. Summarising a chapter method**

It involves gaining in-depth understanding of the contents of a chapter of the Bible through careful reading, responding to general matter related to the content, and summarising the central ideas of the passage.

1. Choose titles for the chapter/paragraphs.
2. Describe/summarise the chapter in your own words.
3. List the main characters in the chapter.
4. Choose what you think the key verse in the chapter is.

5. Write down the key words from the chapter.
6. List the difficulties.
7. Relate the passage to other references (other examples).
8. Outline what you learn from God in the chapter.
9. Write down the central idea of the chapter.
10. Apply

**3. Verse by verse method**

It involves choosing a passage from Scripture and examining it in detail, asking questions of it, finding references, and paraphrasing each verse. For each verse, a personal and measurable application is found.

1. Choose a passage.
2. Read it verse by verse.
3. Write a personal paraphrase of the verse.
4. Write down some questions, answers, and observations.
5. Look for references for each verse.
6. Note down any other findings or conclusions on the verse.
7. Write a personal application.

**4. Bible study method**

Try and answer the following questions:

1. What does the Bible say? (Observation)
2. What is the Bible trying to say? (Interpretation)
3. What does the Bible want to say to me? (Application)

**5. *Lectio Divina***

Read the text through various times, in a contemplative way. The first time is a simple reading; the second time, meditate on some of the words or phrases that caught your attention; the third time, pray about what caught your attention; the fourth time, receptively contemplate on the Lord.

**6. Other methods**

- Thematic method
- Terminological method
- Character method

- Have you used any of these methods to draw close to the Word?
- What was your experience?
- Do you know of any other methods? Which ones?

## Making the most of the opportunities that the context offers

It is unavoidable that our numerous contexts, both cultural and subcultural, affect our daily ministry. When we see them as opportunities, instead of as threats or challenges, they significantly increase our ministry potential.

### *Pre-understandings*

It is important that we examine the influence our preunderstandings have on the way we draw near to the Word and make use of it. All our actions stem from a series of beliefs and pre-understandings. These are often subconscious, which means we cannot always articulate what we believe, even though our actions reflect those beliefs. "Every reader has a worldview, and so every reader comes to Scripture with an 'interpretive grid' that predisposes that reader to see and hear certain things in the Bible" (Brown 2007, 122). Recognising and understanding our pre-understandings requires a high degree of awareness. They are sometimes so deeply rooted that we are not even aware of the fact that they are leading us to a predetermined interpretation and, consequently, could cause us to lose the gift of being more enriched and/or challenged.

### Food for Thought

- Can you think of any pre-understandings among the people you serve?
- Can you think of any pre-understandings you have?
- How would you classify them?
- How do you think they affect reading the Word?
- How does being more aware of your pre-understandings help you?

Preunderstandings can be divided into three categories: doctrinal, inherited, and experiential. First, doctrinal pre-understandings are the ones that are directly derived from our theological context – how we have been trained theologically. For example, the fact that we value

Scripture as a set of pre-understandings: we approach it, searching for well-organised, systematic compartments in order to discover everything it has to tell us regarding faith and the way we believe God asks us to live.

Second, inherited pre-understandings include cultural pre-understandings, which include our ecclesiastic sub-cultures. In some cases, they are easy to identify – for example, the fact that we usually read the Bible through a Western lens, or we adopt a traditional stance on a woman's role because that is what we have inherited from both our culture and our ecclesiastic tradition. Other cases are more subtle, such as the fact that we approach the Bible with the baggage of tradition, like the belief that the Bible is holy. Another inherited pre-understanding could be an imposed baggage: we believe that we are expected to approach the Word a certain way because the pastor "is always right" when they preach or because we belong to such-and-such a denomination.

Third, experiential pre-understandings are the ones we have constructed through drawing near to the biblical text with varying degrees of success. For example, when we approach Scripture with an attitude of, "I already know this" or, "the Bible has nothing to say on this subject" or, "I can't understand that". These kinds of attitudes can lead to the belief that we need an expert in order to read and understand Scripture, for example. Or the opposite, that we don't need anyone. Additionally, the way in which the Bible is presented can influence how we understand it: it can encourage us to draw nearer to it or it provokes rejection.

It is crucial that we are aware of our own pre-understandings because this will determine how we use or present the Bible. But it is just as important that we help the people we serve to be aware of their pre-understandings, or we run the serious risk of them hearing what they want to hear. This attitude puts their process of transformation in grave danger.

### *Methods and programmes*

Studying the Word is done individually, but also in groups and in many different ways. When it comes to methodologies, however, there is an intense polarisation of opinions and feelings. Some leaders stress the importance of these, insisting that using them produces results. Naturally, others swing to the other extreme and are routinely suspicious of any type of methodology and discard them all completely. This is often, whether consciously or not, the result of a desire for control. For example, any biblical approach that prioritises the cognitive aspect is naturally inclined toward information rather than transformation. It can be useful, but it can be clearly seen when, for example, the Bible is used to enter into heated debates just for the sake of arguing. The goal is more likely to be proving who is right instead of seeking common enrichment and growth. Another example is when there is always time to understand the text, but little or no time to apply it.

There is an underlying danger when the method that should help us position ourselves for transformation actually focuses more on the technique rather than the method itself. When methodology is reduced to a technique, it quickly becomes routine that eventually leads to boredom and staleness. The consequences are very sad because people lose their motivation to draw near to the living Word of God and, what's worse: "If we reduce the Bible to a tool to be used, the tool builds up calluses in our hearts" (Peterson 2011, 92). If methodology is a tool, then it should be used in the right way. But, at the same time, one should not be inflexible in using methodologies. We must be free to adapt them according to what is needed. Going one step further, we should be willing to regularly evaluate their use in order to discern whether they are still relevant or adequate and consider the impact they are having on the lives of the people we serve. Methods do not transform people, the Holy Spirit does. However, a method is a channel that helps us position ourselves so that the Spirit moves in our lives.

Tools and resources, such as commentaries, concordances, and dictionaries should not be substitutes that obstruct our own reflection and understanding of the text, or that make our minds think about what so-and-so said. On the contrary, the absence of resources can be just as damaging since it can lead to an individualistic and mistaken interpretation of the text. The same thing happens with the use of different translations: we should promote modern translations of the Bible that people can easily understand.

## Food for Thought

- What type of resources do you use to study the Word?
- How can they hinder your reading?
- How do they help you?

Allowing God to transform us takes time. It is true that we cannot influence time, but we can change our attitude towards it. To start with, we must choose to be subject to and led by the Holy Spirit instead of by anxiousness over a deadline or finishing a particular programme. Furthermore, we must make the most of all the learning opportunities that may present themselves to us, instead of getting carried away by the expectation of what should happen within a certain amount of time. And, therefore, there must also be a long-term commitment to the follow-up and guidance that is necessary to establish habits that go beyond mastering a technique or a methodology. Although we can be useful tools in God's hands, our motivation should not be to make disciples that depend on us to understand and handle the Word and plan their study routines. Lastly, our mission is to be channels so that approaching the Word becomes something enjoyable that leads to dependence on its heavenly Teacher.

### *Postmodernism versus modernism*

Postmodernism questions the truth and relevance of the story. We can see its influence on believers, for example, in their need to find answers to questions that focus on appeasing ethical doubts that they face day after day, rather than abstract questions. In other words, they need to find an answer to why there is suffering – or doubt, which is generally the result of their own painful experiences – rather than the question of whether or not Jesus was a historic figure. Questions that are related to defining an objective truth can seem too abstract, irrelevant, or impossible to understand. There is reason, therefore, to question our methods, which are more likely to fit in with mental and linear approaches that emphasise preconceived ideas and the definition of an objective truth. Nowadays, people do not necessarily believe, understand, or identify with arguments that are painstakingly thought-out; that is, they will not necessarily respond to an approach to the Bible that is guided by rigid parameters. Therefore, we must ask ourselves whether our motivations for using them are actually guided by a need for control, or a desire to play it safe or feel more comfortable.

Ideally, we would choose to make use of the opportunities that a formational use of the Bible presents us with in this context, such as using stories. People want and need stories because, by identifying with them, we do not just discover the answers to our everyday questions, but we also find in them empathy and a source of solace and hope. But even more eloquently, stories also allow us to meet a God who reveals Himself, who reveals His story of redemption - His Great Story. This Great Story, which we are invited into, is where we can find our true place. This is where we satisfy our need for answers to all our daily questions and where we find the necessary encouragement to walk the path of faith. This is where we come home.

In the Gospels specifically, we find that they do not just tell stories that we can identify with, but rather, through knowing the words of the sacred text, they also invite us to encounter the Word that became flesh. What can at first seem to be a search for an abstract truth becomes an encounter with Truth personified. We encounter Jesus in a fresh new way and, through the Gospels, we encounter the One who models what we long to be.

## EXERCISE

Ask someone to read you the following passage and "listen" to it – a first time with your "eyes"; a second time, with your "ears"; a third time, with your "emotions":

> Now that same day two of them were going to a village called Emmaus, about seven miles from Jerusalem. They were talking with each other about everything that had happened. As they talked and discussed these things with each other, Jesus himself came up and walked along with them; but they were kept from recognizing him.

He asked them, "What are you discussing together as you walk along?" They stood still, their faces downcast. One of them, named Cleopas, asked him, "Are you the only one visiting Jerusalem who does not know the things that have happened there in these days?" "What things?" he asked. "About Jesus of Nazareth," they replied. "He was a prophet, powerful in word and deed before God and all the people. The chief priests and our rulers handed him over to be sentenced to death, and they crucified him; but we had hoped that he was the one who was going to redeem Israel. And what is more, it is the third day since all this took place. In addition, some of our women amazed us. They went to the tomb early this morning but didn't find his body. They came and told us that they had seen a vision of angels, who said he was alive. Then some of our companions went to the tomb and found it just as the women had said, but they did not see Jesus."

He said to them, "How foolish you are, and how slow to believe all that the prophets have spoken! Did not the Messiah have to suffer these things and then enter his glory?" And beginning with Moses and all the Prophets, he explained to them what was said in all the Scriptures concerning himself.

As they approached the village to which they were going, Jesus continued on as if he were going farther. But they urged him strongly, "Stay with us, for it is nearly evening; the day is almost over."

So he went in to stay with them. When he was at the table with them, he took bread, gave thanks, broke it and began to give it to them. Then their eyes were opened and they recognized him, and he disappeared from their sight. They asked each other, "Were not our hearts burning within us while he talked with us on the road and opened the Scriptures to us?" They got up and returned at once to Jerusalem. There they found the Eleven and those with them, assembled together and saying, "It is true! The Lord has risen and has appeared to Simon." Then the two told what had happened on the way, and how Jesus was recognized by them when he broke the bread. (Luke 24:13-35)

- How does this experience make reading the passage richer?

- How does this reading refresh your relationship with Jesus?

***The media and social networks***

Nowadays, everyone has access to training, but this has also led to a lowering of the quality of teaching. Added to this, and which is even more significant, there is the influence of the media. In general, the result is that people read less, think less (or at least, think less for themselves), and mainly express themselves through social media. Therefore, the reality is that the people we serve reflect a diverse array of intellectual abilities – some will have had more opportunities than others; some will be more intellectually endowed than others, independently of the level of training they have received. However, we continue to primarily guide their approach to the Bible with intellectual methods, ignoring the fact that not all of them have the necessary intellectual ability, curiosity, or interest, and that on top of this, all of them live under the influence of the media and social media.

## Reading as a community

We are currently faced with a society in which individualism has prevailed, and this reality has been exacerbated by the considerable and increasing use of social media. This individualism is reflected in the fact that we prioritise competitiveness over cooperation, personal interest over common interest, private life and faith over a shared experience, and impersonal or virtual relationships over genuine relationships. Regarding the main subject of this chapter, we see the influence of individualism in our everyday ministry when, for example, people lack commitment when it comes to studying the Word as part of a group. They easily justify themselves by saying that the activity in question is not of personal interest to them nor is it a priority, or that they do not have time. We should listen to these reasons and give them the attention they are due. But we must also see whether these reasons are excuses that may hide weightier reasons. We want to invite people to an experience that goes beyond simply studying the Bible as a group in order to learn facts and fill their minds with information, because we believe that through the Word they will encounter the God who moulds and transforms them.

If we want to guide the people we serve so that they encounter the God of the Word, we must create communities in which people feel safe, so that the experience is a positive, and above all transforming, one. We will dive into this subject in chapter 7 ("The Learning Community"), but it is important that we reflect on some of the aspects that are directly related to the subject we are currently discussing: the Word that shapes us.

When we create safe communities, we minimise situations that may cause resistance to change. For example, if a person feels challenged or even forced to open up and share in a group, without feeling safe, their resistance may increase; they may feel the pressure and end up sharing, but that does not mean that their intention is necessarily to put into practice what they shared. Under these circumstances, it is easy to trivialise applying the Word to our lives - if a person considers it to not be anyone's business and that matters related to faith are meant to be kept private and are not for sharing with the group. The consequence of this is that the person will be excluded from the responsibility of being accountable. This resistance will only increase if there is also no true commitment to growing together as a community, or there is no system in place for accountability and follow-up, or if there are pressing scheduling issues that lead to avoiding everything that commitment implies.

People will also tend to reject any activity with a formal, class-like format, or any format that invites a more passive or even absent attitude. Their interest, their need even, hinges on participating in a gathering that can satisfy their social, emotional, and spiritual needs, rather than just their intellectual needs. These needs are an opportunity to attract them to an authentic community. Within our safe communities, they can seek shelter in order not just to satisfy their needs, but also to be invited on their own journey of transformation. In this way, these spaces become an excellent opportunity to draw close to the Word in order to discover it and grow together. Namely, applying the Word will be a project of communal commitment that involves the whole heart.

Foster says that "The goal of reading the Bible for spiritual transformation is to be changed in order to experience more of life with God. This change occurs in the context of community. Nowhere in Scripture is it suggested that we are lone rangers in the spiritual life" (Foster 2010, 101. Kindle Edition). We must recover the old idea of reading and interpreting Scripture together. Together, we can mutually illuminate and protect each other in order to find the true sense of the text and not stray from it. In this way, we can help each other be accountable and encourage each other to obey Scripture and put it into practice every day. When we live in the Word together, we can have a greater impact in our broken world. Change takes time, but a safe community offers a protective wall and a source of comfort and encouragement, in which the challenge of love offers a space to faithfully traverse the pilgrimage. In this communal context, the invitation should be threefold: listen to God together, obey together, and be held accountable by one another so that we can impact the world.

## Conclusion

God is God; we are not. God does not necessarily ask us to master the passage in order to understand it. However, He does invite us to accept the mystery and live lives of obedience according to what we do know: "The secret things belong to the Lord our God, but the things revealed belong to us and to our children forever, that we may follow all the words of this law" (Deuteronomy 29:29). The knowledge that the Word is alive and active (Hebrews 4:12) and the invitation to "study the Scriptures diligently" (John 5:39) opens the door to knowing the One who has the power to transform us – and who does.

Up to this point we have studied the subject from a biblical-theological perspective, and we have turned to spiritual means – the Word and the Holy Spirit – that we naturally receive when we commit to teaching in a way that seeks to transform people. Starting in the following chapter, we will present some of the pedagogical materials that are at our disposal to achieve that goal of transformation. I propose a critical view that will help us compare these resources in light of the Scriptures and God's purpose.

# Chapter 5

## Integral Formation

> As responsible theological educators, we can no longer accept the status quo of an imbalanced cognitively oriented education that is founded on the faulty epistemology of modernist objectivism. The challenge is before us to seek a holistic multidimensional approach to learning that alone can lead us on the path to excellence in curricular development. (Shaw 2014, 76-77)

As we mentioned in chapter 1, the crisis in theological education requires a more holistic and permanent solution. A holistic pedagogical approach to education offers a potential way out because it tries to truly reconcile the chasm between theory and practice, which, as we mentioned before, is one of the main reasons for this crisis. What's more, a paradigm shift from pedagogy centred on the professor to pedagogy centred on the student will enable there to be change in the daily practices of education. But a holistic approach to learning that will lead to transformation does not happen by introducing separate activities and events that deal with academic, spiritual, or practical aspects, respectively. Rather, it happens when we seek to integrate all of them. Throughout this chapter, my invitation is that we consider how we integrate aspects such as theoretical knowledge, spiritual formation, and practical training into our teaching.

### Integration across the triad of "academic, spiritual, and practical formation"

Harkness says, "The scope of education must go beyond a restrictive cognitive qualification to more integrated human development" (Harkness 2001, 145), and Cheesman appropriates the concept of perichoresis[1] to explain the need for the triad purpose of theological education to remain

---

[1] Perichoresis is a Christian theological concept that refers to the degree of union between the persons of the Trinity. The "being in" of the persons among themselves: it implies the way in which the Father is in the Son and the Son in the Father; the Father is in the Holy Spirit, and so on and so forth (Wikipedia – translated from Spanish page).

not only in balance, in terms of status between the three aspects, but interpermeated and not separated (Cheesman 2009, 5). Palmer subscribes to the triadic approach and adds that integrative education brings objective learning to subjective personal assimilation, which students are to be invited to both an inner journey and an outer journey (Palmer, Scribner and Zajonc 2010, 49). He contends that knowledge understood only in a "rational, linear, and controlled manner" and the hanging on to traditional educational worldviews (Palmer, Scribner and Zajonc 2010, 36) contribute to a poor, incomplete, and detrimental way of understanding learning. Conversely, striving for wholeness that includes allowing emotions, prompting ethical thinking and action, and providing experiences, is equally or even more conducive to learning. This is no easy feat, but that should not be an excuse to deter intentionality and systematicity to make it happen. Integrating education should not be an appendix to the overall student's formational experience, but an integral part of the curriculum (Coe 2000, 85; Palmer, Scribner and Zajonc 2010, 2). In other words, when we teach, we must make sure that we do not just reach the mind (knowledge), the heart (spiritual formation), and hands (practice), rather we must make sure that these aspects are integrated into our teaching.

### *Integration across the whole being*

In chapter 2, we considered the fact that people's transformation should affect their entire being. There should be no distinction between the mental and physical body, between mind and heart. Even so, and as we have already pointed out, there is a substantial chasm within the educational context, which can specifically be seen in the fact that there is more focus on teaching than on learning. The focus is on teaching that appeals primarily to cognition and ignores other areas, such as emotions, passions, and desires, or even other ways of learning, such as experiences.

The chasm can also be observed in teaching that appeals to senses less exposed to everyday reality. Witherington mentions the fact that teaching is mostly cognitive but also oral, and appeals therefore to the auditory sense, even though nowadays students respond better to visual stimulation. He suggests: "Something more all-encompassing – appealing to the emotions as well as the mind, to the will as well as the intellect, to the desire to see as well as the need to hear – is required" (Witherington 2005, 38).

## ADDITIONAL RESOURCES

Integrating our mind

In his book *Mindsight: the new science of personal transformation*, Daniel Siegel summarises in nine points the need to integrate our mind in order to lead a healthy life:

**1. Integration of Consciousness**. Body, mental/emotional, relational, and external awareness. Openness to things as they are.

**2. Bilateral Integration**. The left and right hemispheres of the brain work in harmony. The left hemisphere is logical and linear, very literal. The right one is more creative, metaphorical, and symbolic.

**3. Vertical Integration.** The whole body, including the marginal nucleus of the spinal cord, from the brain stem to the mesencephalon (hippocampus) to inside the cerebral cortex.

**4. Memory Integration.** Integrating implicit and explicit memory. When trauma becomes part of the implicit memory, we get stuck in the past. To integrate memory, we turn implicit memories into explicit ones.

**5. Narrative Integration.** Integrating biographical memory. Facing trauma instead of running from it.

**6. State Integration.** We are manifold beings sharing one body. We need to honour our different states: internal, inter-states – different needs that can be present at the same time and which we need to be aware of – and interpersonal states. Maintaining my own states in relation to others.

**7. Interpersonal Integration.** Honouring and supporting each other's differences promotes neural integration in the brain. Communicating emotions, not just about emotions, can be a way of integrating the mind.

**8. Temporal Integration.** Making maps of time. Connecting the narrative. Being aware of our own death. We need to differentiate ourselves before we connect, and we need to recognise the chaos before we can integrate.

**9. Transpirational Integration.** We become aware of our interconnection. Integrating the integration.

This approach both challenges us and confirms that our pedagogical approaches cannot be purely cognitive.

### *Integration through community*

> Integrative education begins with the premise that we are embedded in a communal reality and then proceeds to an epistemological assertion: we cannot know this communal reality truly and well unless we ourselves are consciously and actively in community with it as knowers. (Palmer, Scribner and Zajonc 2010, 27)

Teaching and learning have largely operated individualistically (Dykstra 1991, 35). First, at the level of curricula. Over time, subjects and disciplines have been selected in such a way that they are more representative of tradition than a response to equipping for the real needs of students and their fields of ministry (Grainger 1994, 69-71; Harkness 2001, 143; Liefield and Cannell 1992, 240-241). Some maintain that a wide variety of disciplines should be included in teaching (Grainger 1994, 71-74), whilst others disagree, saying that the important thing is to have subjects that respond to students' needs and prepare them for ministry (Harkness 2001, 149). Each of these approaches have their positive aspects, but disciplines and subjects should be taught while taking into account cross-pollination.[2]

---

[2] This term means that courses should not necessarily be taught by one professor; rather, other professors could be invited to lecture, who with their specialisation and knowledge, will enrich and contribute to the course. Lecturers collaborate with each other in the students' favour and for a more complete and richer course.

EXAMPLE

> I have been at numerous conferences about teaching seminars or workshops. Usually, subjects are assigned according to affinity, but on one occasion I was also assigned a colleague, so that we could develop the seminar together. In the past, my experience with these types of collaborations had been quite negative, probably due to "group work" at school and university that, although it consisted in producing a collaborative project, in the end was always reduced to dividing up the work and assigning a part to each member of the group. Later, we would stick it all together, often in a disjointed way. I always felt this practice was unfair: the group received the same mark, without taking into account each person's work. I always believed I was doing more than the other and yet, my work was not valued!
>
> Nevertheless, on this occasion, the experience was very different! When my colleague and I discussed how we would carry out the work, we realised that we could do it by each contributing what we knew well. This would be our strength! At first, he worked primarily on the content aspects and I worked on the methodology aspects. Then, we both contributed to enriching what the other had already worked on and we delivered the seminar together, once more, according to our strengths. For me, this was a good example of "cross-pollination", one in which we collaborated for a greater good.

This approach combats individualism and isolated silos of knowledge and facilitates mutual enrichment: "Too often scholars do not know what is going on in other fields and do not attempt to relate their studies to other disciplines" and "students [...] are sometimes left to make the connections for themselves" (Grainger 1994, 69). The outcome driven curriculum, an idea we will further develop later on in the chapter, is the key tool for the integration of disciplines (Shafroth 2012, 5).

Second, the focus on the individual also affects teachers. In the best of cases, tenures and academic freedom have led to stagnation and, in the worst of cases, fomenting personal interests instead of seeking the best for the student's learning (Kohl 2009, 153; Cannell 2006, 289). This is then easily reproduced at other levels. For example, when planning training in the local church, we focus on our interests before the interests or needs of the believers we are meant to train. As we stated previously, one way of integrating academic and practical disciplines[3] is through teamwork in which teachers find ways to enrich and contribute to the course in favour of a greater good. This facilitates and enhances learning (Liefield and Cannell 1992, 249-250; Palmer, Scribner and Zajonc 2010, 10).

### FOOD FOR THOUGHT

- Consider a session you have taught or one in which you participated as a listener. How could the subject be enriched by collaborating with others or through other people's intervention?

Ideally, the teacher's role is the one of facilitator, co-leader, and director of the process rather than the one who imparts knowledge top-down (Cannell 2006, 283; Harkness 2001, 145-146; Downs 1994, 79; Palmer, Scribner and Zajonc 2010, 29-30). If the overarching objective for teachers is to see lives transformed, then they have to encourage students to be aware of the presence of the Holy Spirit and respond in obedience to His direction. Not only this, but teachers must also leave room for the Holy Spirit to move freely within teaching/learning contexts. This can only happen if they are open and obedient to the work of the Holy Spirit in their lives.

### FOOD FOR THOUGHT

The concept of "teacher facilitator" is key in a pedagogical approach that tries to help the student be responsible for their own learning process (as we will discuss more broadly in the next chapter).

- How do you think this model benefits the student?

[3] Although I question the traditional classification of academic and practical disciplines for the simple reason that all disciplines should lead to a practical result. Every discipline should contribute to students being increasingly transformed according to Christ's image.

- How does this model inspire your own teaching practices? Why?

- What should change about your teaching practices? In other words, how can you become a teacher that transitions from the transmitting information model to the facilitating model?

Institutions and teachers need to focus less on how to maintain the institution for the sake of the institution rather than the students' learning, transformation, and equipping for ministry. They need to stop being satisfied with education based on the transmission of information, where students simply fulfil requirements and earn degrees. They should focus on vocational holiness rather than promoting career idolatry (Peterson 1994, 4).

Third, the focus on individual learning, achievement, and assessment has encouraged competition instead of collaborative learning. However, "research points us to the fact that we learn best through our relationships" (Palmer, Scribner and Zajonc 2010, 104). It is no longer true that the teacher is the "sole custodian of knowledge" (Jaison 2015, 6). Students learn from teachers, teachers learn from students, and students learn from their peers, as we will see in detail in chapter 7.

### *Integration through a new pedagogical paradigm*

> Almost every major book or article on the topic of renewal in theological education mentions the problem of a theory-practice dichotomy. (Cannell 2006, 290)

Integrative education is needed to bridge the gap between theory and practice. Palmer argues: "The conventional pedagogy persists because it conveys a view of reality that simplifies our lives" (Palmer 1993, 39). The excuses teachers offer, such as not having time to think about pedagogical issues (Harkness 2008, 185), their inclination towards academic education rather than professional and practical instruction

(Aleshire 2008, 23), professors' interests (Kohl 2009, 153), or other well-articulated reasons, do not seem to be convincing anymore:

> Our resistance to community undermines faculty growth as well as student learning, especially when it comes to the evolution of pedagogy. There is no reason why the academy is still 'delivering' most of its 'product' in lecture form, a pedagogy that originated because books were rare and most people could not read. (Palmer, Scribner and Zajonc 2010, 44)

If we want to see improvements in learning, we need practical pedagogical models that confirm the theory. True transformation will not happen by merely transmitting information.

## Food for Thought

- Think about the day-to-day of your ministry. What informal spaces or moments present themselves?
- How can you be intentional about incorporating them as training opportunities?
- In what way?

We must incorporate or enhance non-formal opportunities as valid forms of learning (Collinson 2004, 233; Ninan 2010, 4; Cannell 2006, 334; Shaw 2014, 107), fostering student involvement and activeness in embracing their own learning. We must incorporate a variety of teaching methodologies:[4] simulations, case studies, interviews, class discussions, small group discussions, brainstorming, forums, encounters, use of sensorial resources,

[4] A good resource for delving deeper into this subject is the book by Marlene LeFevre, *Creative Teaching Methods. How to be an Effective Teacher.* English version published in 2013 by David C. Cook Publishing Company.

debates, the use of questions, etc. (Downs 1994, 155-195; Harkness 2001, 147; Parker 1993, 69; Shaw 2014, 181-200; Wanak 2010, 290).

FOOD FOR THOUGHT

- Consider the different teaching methods you have experienced or used for your teaching practice. How have they helped you?
- How have they helped your students learn?

In a way, the challenge is in our hands despite the work it implies:

> An integrative approach to teaching and learning can get messy. But it gets no messier than life itself and, done well, can help bring order to chaotic raw experience, as is the case with any well-crafted cycle of action and reflection. The real question is whether we want higher education to be about life. (Palmer, Scribner and Zajonc 2010, 36)

One way of accepting the challenge of promoting a pedagogy of integration is by means of a model of pedagogy via objectives.

FOOD FOR THOUGHT

- Looking at the various levels of integration, which one challenges you the most? Why? How will you incorporate it into your teaching practice?

### *Outcome-based approach pedagogy*

The university world in Europe went through an important reform as a result of the Bologna Declaration in 1999 that was signed by 29 countries and established "a common European Higher Education Area" (EHEA). "The overall aim is to improve the efficiency and effectiveness of higher education in Europe" (Kennedy, Hyland and Ryan 2012, 2). One of the important outcomes of the Declaration was the implementation of course learning outcomes:

> Learning outcomes are important for recognition [...] The principal question asked of the student or the graduate will therefore no longer be "what did you do to obtain your degree?" but rather "what can you do now that you have obtained your degree?" This approach is of relevance to the labour market and is certainly more flexible when taking into account issues of life-long learning, non-traditional learning, and other forms of non-formal educational experience. (Purser, Council of Europe 2003, 2)

This means that we need education that equips the students for well beyond their stage of education. Therefore, the curriculum must respond to the context, and the learning objective must be designed taking into account what the student needs to understand and move around in the context. Additionally, the context is constantly changing and, consequently, we must teach students to learn how to adapt to these changing contexts. In chapter 6, we will take a more detailed look at the need for understanding students in their context.

Learning outcomes are part of the outcome-based approach pedagogy found in an educational paradigm change that moves from a traditional instructional paradigm, or a teacher-centred approach, to a student or learner-centred approach. Instructional pedagogy revolves around the teacher, who is the expert and the main keeper and communicator of knowledge. "For some, this remains the essence of education; it is the handing of a tradition from the wise to the learner [...] learning remains essentially top down" (Wingate 2003, 242). The student becomes the recipient of the knowledge communicated. One of the important drawbacks to this approach is that educational success is measured on the instructor's performance and the instructional content rather than on the student's real learning. A few decades ago, Le Bar was already questioning the traditional approach, and his words encapsulate well the need for a paradigm shift: "What is teaching but helping people to learn? Therefore, the basic problem is not teaching, but learning" (Le Bar 1958, 135). In other words, the fact that a teacher has taught does not necessarily mean that a student has learned: "A pupil's growth is determined not by what he hears, but by what he does about what he hears" (Le Bar 1958, 136).

As Christian teachers, we ought to be concerned both for our students' spiritual growth and for their acquisition of information or cognitive knowledge. The goal is not only to know about God but to know God. As stated in chapter 2, the transformation of a Christian, even though it is a process that will only end in glory, ought to be real and visible, springing from the inside and out. "True learning has outward manifestations, yet they will not represent real and permanent changes unless something has first happened inside. The truth of God must progressively control the inner life" (Le Bar 1958, 144). A life that responds to what has been taught is the proof of true learning.

Shafroth, in her study of "Learner-Centered Management at Theological Seminaries", identifies five main characteristics of the learner-centred pedagogy: 1) balance of power (teachers share classroom control by empowering the students to be involved in their own learning process), 2) responsibility for learning (students not only take ownership of their own learning but they do it in community and peer learning), 3) function of content (the emphasis is not on the amount of material covered by lecturing but on how much students learn), 4) the role of the teacher (the teacher becomes a facilitator of learning rather than an instructor of knowledge), and finally, 5) purpose and process of evaluation (the students' assessment on learning is not based on grades but on the achievement of learning outcomes) (Shafroth 2012, 2-8). She also states, in the context of theological education:

> When a seminary wants to become more learner-centered, the mission of the seminary changes from providing instruction to producing learning, whereby the college takes responsibility for student learning and not just for providing teaching. (Shafroth 2012, 8)

Theological education institutions in Europe have had to adhere to the changes established by Bologna. Nowadays, courses and assessments are designed with learning outcomes, yet some theologians have pointed out that learning outcomes have often been ill-designed (Cannell 2006, 306; Shaw 2014, 145). Therefore, two important questions need to be asked: What are the learning outcomes and how can they be designed in order to be as effective as possible?

Kennedy, Hyland, and Ryan, in their Bologna implementation document, conclude by saying that the two main common elements are: "Learning outcomes focus on what the learner has achieved rather than the intentions of the teacher and learning outcomes focus on what the learner can demonstrate at the end of a learning activity" (Kennedy, Hyland and Ryan 2012, 5). Verghese adds the idea that an objective, or learning outcome, "is an action-oriented statement of instructional intent" (Verghese 2010, 1). Shaw suggests giving consideration to the following questions prior to designing learning outcomes: "Why should the students care about this lesson enough to engage with me in significant learning? How might this lesson help emerging leaders in their preparation for ministry?" (Shaw 2014, 166). Fink offers the following to consider in terms of learning outcomes:

> What is important for them to learn and retain, 2-3 years after the course is over? What kind of thinking or application abilities do you want them to develop? How do you want them to keep on learning after the course is over? (Fink 2003, 4)

Bloom's taxonomy is widely used to design learning outcomes. "He identifies three domains of learning – cognitive, affective and psycho-motor" (Kennedy, Hyland and Ryan 2012, 7). Ziegler, mentioned by Verghese, picks up this classification and contextualises it in the field of theological education, specifying the following domains: cognitive (Scripture exegesis, intellectual reference, academic disciplines for teaching, doctrinal knowledge, scholarly research), affective (to help with spiritual growth), psycho-motor (to equip for practical ministry) (Verghese 2010, 4). It is important, at this point, to realise that Bloom's taxonomy and Ziegler's contextualisation are a reflection of the Bible colleges' triad purpose of academic instruction, spiritual formation, and ministry training. It should also be recognised how these taxonomies, within this new instructional paradigm, are assets designed to better maintain the original triad on track. All three areas are important, and all three areas need to be reflected in curriculum content design and teaching methodologies. More importantly, they provide the platform for an integrative evaluation of the student's learning, as will be demonstrated later. Fink provides an interesting model with an alternative classification, based on a learning-centred approach. He proposes a taxonomy of significant learning:

> When students and teachers think about what students can learn that is truly significant, their answers usually include, but do not focus on, 'understand and remember' kinds of learning. More often they emphasize such things as critical thinking, learning how to creatively use knowledge from the course, learning to solve real-world problems,

> changing the way students think about themselves and others, realizing the importance of life-long learning, etc. (Fink 2003, 8)

This taxonomy includes:

> Foundational knowledge, understanding and remembering information and ideas; application, skills, critical, creative and practical thinking; integration, connecting ideas, people, realms of life; human dimension, learning about oneself and others; caring, developing new feelings, interests and values; learning how to learn, becoming a better student, inquiring about a subject, self-directing learners. (Fink 2003, 9)

It is a compelling taxonomy because it goes beyond Bloom's in several aspects that, if implemented, facilitate students' learning. It indicates that students are not blank slates but come to class not only with a backpack full of previous knowledge and experiences, but also with factors that can facilitate or hinder their learning. It is not only essential to know the individual – "It will be good to know with what sort of learners we are dealing and then try to figure out how to reach them" (Witherington 2005, 38) – but also for the individual to be self-aware. It invites a much more holistic approach, where all aspects of the individual are important and taken into consideration in the process of learning. It is not only about ensuring cognitive assimilation, "it is about capturing the imagination" (Witherington 2005, 38), the "formation of hearts and desires" (Smith 2009, 18), and appealing to the whole being. Finally, it recognises that learning is a life-long process, thus suggesting that equipping students is not only for them to acquire learning but to help them acquire the tools for learning, and learn how to learn for life, which is the subject of chapter 8.

## How to write effective learning objectives

The key to writing effective learning objectives is the verbs that are used to formulate them. They must be action verbs, given that the goal is that students know what they can do at the end of a learning activity.

Bloom's taxonomy notes the verbs that are most used according to the levels of learning. The higher levels aim for higher levels of complexity. The following table focuses on the most common classification: the cognitive area.

| LEVEL OF LEARNING | MOST FREQUENTLY USED VERBS |
|---|---|
| **Level 1: KNOWLEDGE**<br>The expectation is that students remember information, memorise facts and specific terms. | Understand, recognise, know, define, memorise, repeat, list, remember, name, associate (as a list), mention, present, propose, say, identify, perceive, classify, characterise, label... |
| **Level 2: COMPREHENSION**<br>The expectation is that students can summarise or explain in their own words, express ideas, and predict the effects or immediate implications of known facts. | Understand, restate, discuss, describe, recognise, try, explain, express, identify, localise, inform, check, tell, turn into, interpret, present, respond... |
| **Level 3: APPLICATION**<br>The expectation is that students make use of the information, exactly as they received it or in a different way. | Apply, translate, interpret, use, demonstrate, represent, practise, illustrate, operate, programme, outline, associate, prepare, show, begin, influence, express, carry out, meet... |
| **Level 4: ANALYSIS**<br>The expectation is that students can predict a result, generalise, or break down the fundamental parts of an idea, principle, rule, or fact, recognise tacit suppositions and verify their coherence. | Analyse, distinguish, separate, calculate, experiment, try, compare, contrast, critique, map out, inspect, debate, list, ask, connect, resolve, examine, associate, differentiate, outline, adjust, adapt, classify... |
| **Level 5: SYNTHESIS**<br>The expectation is that students create knowledge based off of the information provided by a source or various sources. | Synthesise, compose, plan, propose, design, formulate, order, join, group, compile, gather, build, create, organise, manage, prepare, combine, collect, develop, integrate, modify... |

| Level 6: EVALUATION The expectation is that students can make a value judgment and justify it with coherent reasoning, or that they estimate the value of something, according to certain criteria. | Evaluate, assess, appraise, value, measure, compare, examine, rate, select, choose, estimate, weigh, balance, conclude...[5] |
|---|---|

We must also take into consideration the affective domain. Within this, there are five main categories:

1. Receiving information;
2. Responding: student's participation in their own learning;
3. Valuing: acceptance and commitment to values;
4. Organisation: the process people go through as they bring together different values, resolve conflicts among them, and start to internalise the values;
5. Characterisation: value system that controls behaviour in a consistent and predictable manner (Kennedy, Hyland and Ryan 2012, 9).

The European Council for Theological Education (ECTE – http://ecte.eu) has compiled a list of thirty specific competences for theological education programmes based on the list of generic competences for Higher Education programmes that can be used as a resource for curriculum development (Oxenham, 2010).

There are strong advantages to this pedagogical approach. First, for teachers, it helps them to better define the curriculum, goals for learning, and teaching methodology to achieve learning outcomes, and also to communicate this approach to the students, thus setting clear expectations of what is required of them. Second, it also helps the

[5] There are many resources available on this subject. This table is a translation of the one found on the website of the National University of San Juan, Puerto Rico: http://www.unsj.edu.ar/unsjVirtual/sistema_gestion_calidad/wp-content/uploads/2015/04/Redacciòn-Objetivos-taxonom%C3%ADa-Bloom.P.2.1.9.pdf.

students, clarifying what they can expect from a given class and what is expected of them. And third, it gives the curriculum a better stand for assessment (Kennedy, Hyland and Ryan 2012, 24-27).

## Food for Thought

- Consider a session you have taught or taken part in as a listener. Describe the subject and define two or three learning objectives.

## Exercise

1. *Gather together various curricula* (they can be from theological training courses, training for adults from a church, training programmes, etc.) and analyse them in light of this chapter:
    - Are there any learning objectives? How have they been defined? What areas of learning do they include?
    - What pedagogical approach does the curriculum fit into? Are there any integrating elements?
    - How do they take into account the teacher's contribution? What about the student's?
2. *Design a training plant through assessment*
    - Describe the training elements of your place of ministry (this could be training Sunday school teachers, training adults, preaching, small groups, specific training programmes, leadership training, or others).
    - Carry out an evaluation analysis based on the curricular content of this book.
    - Create a new training proposal.

3. *Design a training subject*
   - Choose a training programme for a group of adults from a church.
   - Design the general objectives for the programme.
   - Develop the structure of the programme. It must contain:
     - Objectives for each section.
     - A summary of the contents of each section.
     - Activities, readings, and other teaching tools that can be used to deliver the training.
   - Design the method by which the programme will be evaluated.

## Conclusion

In this chapter we have presented the integrated education model as an alternative model. This model allows us to critically reflect on our current teaching practices, but it also allows us to understand how we can incorporate the necessary changes for higher efficiency in our teaching and, consequently, allow the transformation of our students.

Up until here we have reflected on how we should reframe not just our pedagogical approach but also our role as teachers, in order to make learning easier for our students. The following chapter is an invitation to reflect on how the individual student should take ownership of their own learning process, and how we can help them do that.

# Chapter 6

## Responsible Learning

> Helping people to know God and to be obedient to him is perhaps the greatest gift we can bestow. (Downs 1994, 27)

Right about the time I was starting to write this chapter, I had the privilege of running part of the programme for an event. I saw this as an occasion to not only teach the participants, but also to train leaders. So, I surrounded myself with a team of volunteers in order to fulfil my mission. I love taking every opportunity that presents itself to apply another important principle: transformation that multiplies, which we will explore further in chapter 8. A month before the event, I got in touch with the group of young people that someone had selected for me, so that we could go over the material and be better prepared. Some responded enthusiastically, others took a bit longer, and some never even got back to me. The reason they gave was mostly a lack of time. Although collaborating with this group is something I look back on fondly, I can't help but smile when I think of the excuses, apologies, or need for approval that I received from various of them throughout the event.

On this occasion, by the grace of God, I was able to respond with forbearance. However, I must confess that it has not always been that way throughout my teaching career. It saddens me to think about how many times my teaching has been exacting, scolding, disparaging, arrogant, and countless other attitudes that not only are not in keeping with what the Lord calls me to be, but also have precisely the opposite effect to stimulating responsible learning.

Grenz concludes his phenomenal book on theology by asking the following question: "Will the vision of God's ultimate future motivate us to be about the work of the triune God in the present era until Christ comes in glory and splendour?" (Grenz 1994, 659). It is a particularly profound question: on the one hand, it reminds us that transformation is carried out by God and that "perfection" or full transformation will not occur until after death. On the other hand, however, it clearly challenges us: although our transformation is carried out by God, it also requires our will, as we discussed in chapter 2. We can narrow this conversation down by asking ourselves, "Why do the students we serve act as if they owed us something?", "Why does one get the impression that they are always the receivers?" or "Why do they only seem to be interested at times rather than consistently?", and a whole host of other reasons that end up putting students in the defendant's chair. But the following reflection is more realistic and relevant for our role as teachers: If students are to be consciously responsible for their own path to maturity, what then is our role? How can we help them on this journey? How can we make sure that they grow in reliance on God and not on us? These are some of the questions we will discuss throughout this chapter.

## The responsible student

FOOD FOR THOUGHT

- Consider the different stages of your education. Which people were influential in motivating you?
- What did they do that motivated you?
- Based on your answers, put together a list of "Motivators for a teaching ministry".

The main reason that will encourage students to journey towards responsible learning lies in the motivations that we find in the Word of God. We ourselves must make them ours if we want to transmit them to the students we serve. We have already touched on these matters in previous chapters, but it is worth picking up some important points once more. First, salvation – which includes conversion and subsequent sanctification, or transformation as I prefer to call it – leads us to union in Christ. We return to the original relationship that God designed at creation. We return to the created order. That relationship is based on God's love for us, so it is functional and/or transactional, and it persuades us to a life of obedience.

We love because He loved us first and that love is what motivates us to strive towards transformation, even though we know that complete transformation will come to fruition in our future glorification. This should be a powerful incentive for those of us who live mediocre spiritual lives and who have given up hope of ever experiencing "something more". The desire to make an effort to be transformed is motivated by the conviction that there is more; as Jesus says, "I have come that they may have life, and have it to the full" (John 10:10).

We must put aside the debate that tries to determine who does what and instead move on to each taking on our own role. Our own effort cannot cause transformation: that is the role of the Holy Spirit, as we determined in chapter 3. Our role is to position ourselves voluntarily and regularly in order to be touched and transformed by God. We must grow in intimacy with Him, and we can do that through prayer and through developing a listening attitude that simply delights in His presence. Spiritual disciplines can help us in this process: "They must never be seen as tasks that a Christian must do in order to grow. They are channels of grace that position us to meet the Lord" (Wardle 2003, 122). They help us choose transformation and live lives of love and obedience. As teachers, we have the privilege of helping students in that process, which will lead them to not only know of God, but also experience God more fully.

## Additional Resources

**Spiritual disciplines**

**Solitude:** choosing to withdraw from daily activities to be alone with God.

**Silence:** choosing to avoid the noise of the world in order to hear God's whispers.

**Fasting:** abstaining from food for a specific period of time in order to lessen the hold the flesh has on our lives and open the way to experiencing the strength of God in the midst of our weakness.

**Secrecy:** following Jesus' admonishment to serve and give privately.

**Sacrifice:** give beyond our ability in response to the God who gives himself.

**Study:** take time to meditate on the Word of God. The goal is not to acquire information but to allow God to transform our lives spiritually.

**Worship:** declare the wonder and supreme value of God, engaging our hearts, minds, souls, and bodies as a continual offering of worship.

**Service:** engage lives, resources, talents, and spiritual gifts to minister to others.

**Prayer:** through the power of the Holy Spirit, have communion with God through prayer and impact the world through intercession.

**Communion:** actively choose to be part of a healthy and spiritual community as a place of strength, growing faith, and love in action. (Wardle 2004, 54)

Second, even though individualism is one of the characteristics of the Western world we live in, this is not God's design. Christian students are not called to live an independent life. They are not even meant to envisage the process of maturity by themselves, rather they must be invited to live in the context of a community in which everyone is committed to each other, to the people of God, as we will dive into in chapter 7. This is one more gift of our union in Christ. Grenz says:

> The way to life comes through the giving of one's own life in relation to Christ. Hence, we come to find our true identity – we come to exemplify our true essence – only as we live out the design and destiny God has for us. This design is that we participate together with others in the community of the followers of Christ. (Grenz 1994, 180)

Students should not walk on their own: they have the resource of community at their disposal. We learn from each other through our victories and through our failures. When one falls down, the other can pick them up. We work together so that our unity may broaden our horizons and enrich us. And when lies poke their heads out, threatening to dishearten us, we can remind each other of the profound truths that reside in God's heart.

## Knowing our students

It is vital that we spend time and effort on getting to know students – both the aspects that characterise them as a group and what is unique to each person we have the privilege of serving. This opens up a window to see at what stage of the development process they find themselves; what cognitive, emotional, and behavioural skills and abilities they have acquired and which ones are missing; what difficulties hinder their learning; what their interests and needs are; and what the motivational factors are that stimulate their learning experience.

First, we must understand that, as human beings, our design includes various stages of development.[1] A person cannot move on to the next stage without mastering the previous one (or if they do, it will be with difficulty). This has nothing to do with abilities, IQ, gender, or other matters. It is simply how God created us. Within the context of education, this means that each one of a person's development phases allows them to acquire and apply certain concepts. It is also important to take into account that we are all different and that, therefore, how or how fast we assimilate them will also be different. This difference does not make someone more or less in any way. It simply has to do with how we have been created.[2] All too often we fall into the mistake of teaching based on our classification of students according to inadequate labels and focusing on content that is usually designed as if we were all the same,[3] without taking into account how God has created each one of us.

---

[1] Although I focus primarily on adult developmental aspects, these principles can also be partially applied to children.

[2] The discussion surrounding 1 Corinthians 12 from chapter 3, "The Holy Spirit as an agent of transformation", should illustrate this point.

[3] A notorious example of this reality is how the education system, even in the Church, classifies people according to age.

When we respect a person's various development phases, as well as their individual rhythms, we facilitate and optimise their learning. What's more, we must take into account that, as human beings, we are constantly growing because we are unfinished products. If we are not static, then why should teaching be? This is especially important when it comes to understanding that discipleship is a lifelong process and, therefore, training should also be so, as we will see in chapter 8.

Second, students come with pre-established learning patterns. Consequently, if a student has followed rigid rules and programmes, they will be lost if they have to take initiative and responsibility for their own learning. If a student has experienced a teaching style in which they were a passive receiver, they may be reluctant to accept a more participative style. A student who is used to memorising will find it harder when they are asked to reflect and articulate an opinion; when a student is used to working individually, they will struggle with group work. As teachers, we must make sure that the changes we want to carry out are received positively rather than met with rejection, suspicion, or even resignation.

## Food for Thought

- Consider one or several of your best learning experiences. Why were they the best?
- What did you learn?
- How did you learn?
- How do you prefer to learn?

Third, students have different learning styles. Kolb summarises them into four large categories – the activists, who prefer a specific experience, tend to talk a lot and want to do things; the pensive ones prefer to observe and reflect, they need more time to think and read; the theorists, who prefer to construct abstract concepts and generalise, they like ideas, theories, diagrams, and connexions; and the pragmatists, who prefer to put what they have learned into practice, like attitude changes and action.

**Kolb's learning cycle**

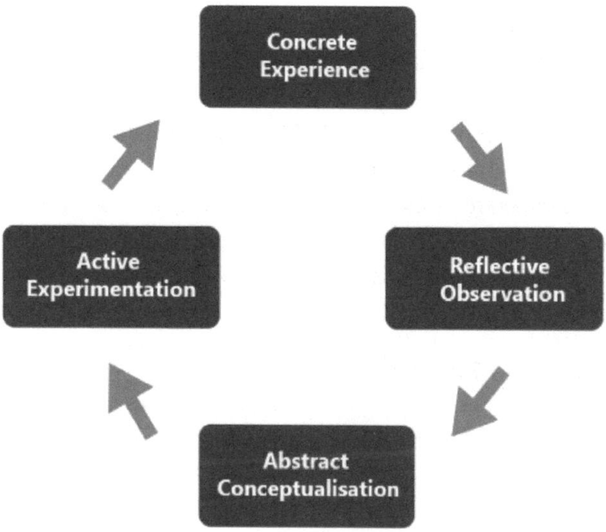


Our tendency is to teach the way we learn, or even to teach in the same way we have been taught, as I mentioned in chapter 3, when I talked about my own experience. But it is precisely because we all learn differently that our training must reflect these different learning styles. What's more, the challenge is even greater given that the student not only learns when they receive training that is adapted to their style, but also when they are challenged to complete the whole learning cycle, which goes through the four types: experimenting (concrete experience), reflecting on the experience (reflective observation), theorising about it (abstract conceptualisation), and practising again in order to experience it better (active experimentation). Learning is also experienced outside of our comfort zone.

Fourth, even though for us, as teachers, teaching is our priority, vocation, passion, and for some even our ministry, this is not necessarily the case for our students, who often arrive with interests or situations that are in competition with their training. This happens primarily in informal learning contexts, such as the training in our churches and ministries. People, and adults in particular, struggle to balance the inevitable tension that exists between all areas of their life: work, family, finances, to name only a few. This tension is not only created by the sacrifice of physical effort and time, but also because it naturally causes emotional fatigue. The worries and realities that come up are endless because they are part of the various stages of life, of living in the world we live in, of the constant struggle we face as sinners. When a student seems to not be paying attention in class, we must ask ourselves whether the problem is a lack of interest,[4] which is what we think all too often, or that their whole being is held up by the fight they had that morning with their teenage son, or that their father is in hospital, or that they do not know how they will pay off their mortgage. Being aware of these realities helps us exercise compassion and care towards the student, to be empathetic. It also invites us to look for the right ways so that the training we are offering radiates passion, is relevant, and connects with their real lives, instead of meeting our own interests and priorities.

## Food for Thought

- Think and write down examples of when your interests or intentions "clashed" with those of your students. How did it make you feel?

- If the student is your priority, how do your intentions reorganise themselves?

[4] It is also important to add that "a lack of interest" is not necessarily the student's responsibility, as we will discuss further on! As teachers, it is our responsibility to capture their interest.

## Involving students in their own learning process

FOOD FOR THOUGHT

- How do students come to the teaching you are about to impart?
- What can you perceive?
- What are the different attitudes?
- What do you think may have provoked that attitude?
- What do you observe regarding a change in attitude from before to after the teaching?
- What do you think causes this change?

### *Identifying needs*

Students often have specific reasons for wanting to learn. Sometimes they can be clearly articulated, but not always. However, even if these intentions are subconscious, they still exert a certain influence. A child's desire to learn may be motivated by curiosity, but their motivation could also be to seek refuge away from a troubled home or to please a demanding parent in order to earn their love. An adult may want to learn in order to improve their job situation, but they could also be motivated by the need to satisfy a dysfunctional and disproportionate desire to be busy or the need to prove their worth as a person. As teachers, it is not only our job to detect these hidden reasons, but we must also work towards persuading students that the main reason we teach is to see their lives transformed into the likeness of Jesus so that their lives impact the world.

As I mentioned previously, students will come to our training programmes with personal interests – especially to the ones in informal contexts. These may be more or less, and consciously or not, connected to their needs. Consequently, our job will involve, on the one hand, identifying these needs and, on the other, reducing the gap between how we as teachers and they as students define them. This is an essential step because how a student defines their needs is often influenced by desires that arise from the pressures of the world we live in, or personal shortcomings that are the result of trauma, immaturity, etc. Therefore, they should not be a priority when it comes to learning. For example, a student may want to improve their biblical knowledge but be motivated by a distorted desire to reach intellectual superiority over others and not by a deep longing for change. A student may want to improve their job situation and be motivated by a desire to improve their purchasing power, but not necessarily by the desire to be more generous. A student may aspire to get good marks, but they are more motivated by winning the professor's approval than by a desire for excellence. A teenager may attend Sunday school because their parents force them to and not because they want to. A person may attend every training event a church has to offer, but their motivation has more to do with doing good works than with a real interest in growing. These ill-defined needs cover up real needs.

### *Identifying obstacles to learning*

FOOD FOR THOUGHT

- What are your fears, challenges, etc. when it comes to learning? Try to categorise them into "obstacles to learning". What is the result?

- What are some of your fears regarding teaching? And regarding your colleagues? What about when it comes to your vocation? How have you dealt with these fears? What have you learned about yourself and about fear?

- What role does fear play in your students' lives? What mechanisms do they use to avoid living encounters with their teachers? What about with challenging subjects? How can teachers help their students to be less afraid?

- Draw three columns on a piece of paper:
  - The title of the first column is "Negative images of students today".
  - The second title is "Fears of students today".
  - The third is "Positive attributes of students today".

- Fill out this table with observations drawn from your own experience.
  - How do these columns relate to each other?
  - How can this profile help you when teaching? (Palmer 2017)

Even though, as teachers, we want to see students transformed, we have to accept that not everyone has had or is having a positive learning experience. Of course, it is true that many experiences that could be considered to be negative can actually be great learning opportunities. However, not everyone is capable of processing and even "repairing" the experiences they perceive as negative in order to draw out the positive and grow from them. Sometimes they are not even willing or prepared to learn. These experiences, which on occasion can be traumatic, result in endless negative consequences. Before we can smooth out the path to learning, and to the consequent growth and maturity of our students, we must identify what causes bumps in the road. First, we could talk about internal causes, such as any type of wound or trauma and crises of faith; and second, external causes, which could be unfavourable physical situations in both the person themselves or their environment, such as a disturbance in room temperature, groups that are too numerous, bad acoustics, poor vision or hearing, for example.

If people respond to learning as a threat, because of the reasons described above, they will naturally have a negative response to it. This will manifest itself in different ways according to their personality: some will run from any learning situation, others will ignore it, and still others will react with hostility. In the day-to-day of learning, these forms of resistance may present themselves as falling behind, being absent, or abandoning the programme; bad relationships with teachers and classmates, which are also exacerbated by differences in personality, elitism, unresolved issues, lack of encouragement; a lack of interest or even unwillingness to be involved in learning; a negative attitude in general and failure. But they may also appear in ways that are more subtle and, unfortunately, unbeknown to the teacher, such as a lack of motivation, anxiety and fear, or lack of confidence in one's ability to learn, and these can block learning and, consequently, transformation. In order for learning experiences to become opportunities for growth, we must be intentional, seeking to identify these obstacles and smooth out the path in order to facilitate a positive experience.

## ADDITIONAL RESOURCES

> In his book *Healing Care, Healing Prayer*,[5] Terry Wardle proposes the following structure (opposite) to show the effects of trauma and wounds in our life.

[5] Wardle, Terry. 2001. *Healing Care, Healing Prayer. Helping the Broken Find Wholeness in Christ.* Abilene, TX: Leafwood Publishers.

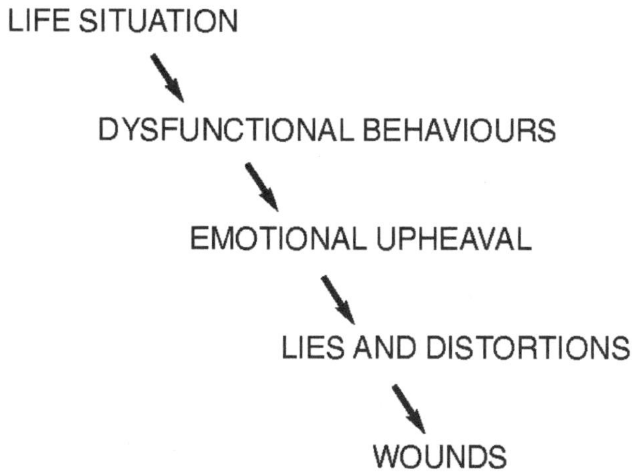


This diagram helps us understand the effects of traumas related to learning experiences or learning itself. If a student suffers from a bad experience – a bad mark, for example – and if those bad experiences are repeated – many bad marks – this can lead to the student starting to believe lies pertaining to their learning skill – for example, "I'm not good at studying", "I'm not good at anything" – which will in turn lead to an irrational and disproportionate emotional response – like an aggressive attitude towards the teacher. This will also result in dysfunctional attitudes – such as absenteeism – which weaken, paralyse, or nullify their chances of learning.

Our empathetic role as teachers is critical in order to provide positive situations that heal and facilitate new paths to receiving learning.

***Building on what is already known***

The idea that students are like a blank page, or a clean slate is a well-established premise that we have often worked with and continue to work with. It is, however, mistaken and untrue. This premise results in us carrying out a form of education that is completely based on what we as teachers can and want to contribute. However, there are three important principles we must remember.

First, students (and this also includes young children), whether we choose to recognise it or not, come with a backpack filled with knowledge, experiences, and values. This entire package is a source of learning which we can influence and build on. Not everything will be positive, constructive, or even mature, which means that our work will have to be orientated towards establishing a firm foundation. In some cases, it will even imply breaking down in order to build back up. However, when this baggage is rich, solid, and appropriate, our contribution will affirm and expand. Building upon what is already known will have a significant exponential role.

Second, Knowles reminds us that "Adults become ready to learn those things they need to know and be able to do in order to cope effectively with their real-life situations" (Knowles, Halton III and Swanson 2005, 67). Simply put, a student will be more inclined to learn if they know that they really will learn and that what they will learn will be useful in their day-to-day life.

Third, "Goal-setting by the learner is important as motivation for learning and personal successes and failures determine how individuals set future goals" (Knowles, Halton III and Swanson 2005, 75). This principle becomes particularly important when we adopt a pedagogy which takes into account the student because it allows us, among other things, to present students with clear learning objectives, as we saw in chapter 5, and because it perfectly encapsulates the idea of responsible learning. As teachers, we cannot impose because then we will not achieve the desired result. If we give students both the space and necessary positive support for them to set their own objectives and help them map out their own road to learning, this will make them owners of their own learning process and lead them to maturity, in accordance with the measure of fullness in Christ.

## Additional Resources

**Motivating the student**

Bruner recommends the following useful questions:

- Are there materials that will stimulate the student's desire to learn? If there are, what are they?

- As a teacher, how can you increase a student's will to learn? What can you do so that students feel like learning the material?
- What is the most effective way of presenting the material?
- Are the learning materials, tools, and other resources appropriate for the student's level?
- What is the presentation sequence?
- What should be given as a reward and when will it be given? How will the training handle students' successes and mistakes?

(Knowles, Halton III and Swanson 2005, 97-98)

## Conclusion

Sometimes we attribute an aimless spiritual life to an inability to understand the mysteries of God but, more often than we would like to admit, there are other reasons involved. It may be laziness, or an unfounded fear of God, or the need to control instead of live dependant on a God who loves us and knows what is best for us. Although God often moves in our lives in ways that are unexpected and contrary to what we hoped, it does not invalidate His invitation to be His partners. Hence the need for students to learn to be responsible for their own path towards transformation.

This morning, I had to ask my son Alex three times to put his shoes on for going to school. When it was time to leave, he was still not ready. When I asked him why they were not on, he said that it was because he liked playing with Legos (which we had agreed he could play with until I asked him to put on his shoes).

What I reflected "post-annoyance" was this: 1) Why did I ask him to put his shoes on? Because I am teaching him to do it on his own, to be responsible. However, I got angry because he disobeyed me. 2) If I am teaching him, it means he is learning; therefore, it is my responsibility to walk alongside him through this learning process. I could have gone downstairs, looked him in the eyes and reminded him about what I asked him to do; I could have helped put the Lego away; I could have sat next to him and encouraged him to put his shoes on; I could have helped him put his shoes on...

In the day-to-day of our ministries there are many examples of things that require our presence and invite us to smooth the way for learning, and consequently for transformation, instead of continuing to amass negative learning experiences. Because, in the end, we are not made or called to make this journey on our own. We need each other, we flourish in community, the community which we are part of in Christ. This is the subject of the next chapter: how the community in Christ becomes a community of learning.

# Chapter 7

## The Learning Community

> Real learning does not happen until students are brought into relationship with the teacher, with each other, and with the subject. We cannot learn deeply and well until a community of learning is created in the classroom. (Palmer 1993, xvi)

The individualistic way in which our society runs is not in line with God's purposes. Believers are called to live within a committed community, the people of God. Grenz says:

> The way to life comes through the giving of one's own life in relation to Christ. Hence, we come to find our true identity – we come to exemplify our true essence – only as we live out the design and destiny God has for us. This design is that we participate together with others in the community of the followers of Christ. (Grenz 1994, 180)

Community is part of God's gracious design to satisfy our innate desire to belong: to be accepted, loved, included, and valued. Its greatest purpose is to provide a platform to help members grow, so that they can reach maturity in Christ. This statement has key implications for our training contexts: these should be within a *community of learning*. And this is what we will explore together throughout this chapter.

### FOOD FOR THOUGHT

- How would you define "community"?
- What do you think a healthy Christian community should be like?
- In what way has your experience of community, both positive and negative, influenced your understanding of Christian community?

## Community as a place of belonging

If we want to understand the reason for and the importance of the community of learning, we must first understand community from a biblical perspective: how it was designed and what for, the effects of it deteriorating, how it is restored, and how it can be protected. Although there are many biblical metaphors that illustrate the concept of community, I would like to extend an invitation to consider the biblical image of the Trinity. Why? Because the sense of community originated from the heart of God, who is inherently communal.

### *The triune God*

God has set the standard from the beginning: the Father has always lived in interrelation with the Son and the Spirit (Genesis 1:26) and has demonstrated what it means to live in a community of love (Matthew 3:16-17). Johnson explains:

> The living God is not a solitary God [...] not an isolated God. From all eternity the living God has lived in relationship – indeed, has lived as relationship. At the center of the universe is relationship. From all eternity the living God has been community, family. (Johnson 2002, 6)

The biggest impact of this trinitarian relationship on our understanding of Christian community is two-fold. First, the act of creation by the triune God in His image cannot be anything other than the creation of human community (Bilezikian 1997, 19) and not of a solitary human being. This truth then leads us to recognise that Christian community is not created by human beings but by God: it is "a divine and spiritual reality" (Bonhoeffer 1954, 26). Therefore, the key element is not so much our exclusive efforts to create, build, and preserve a community, rather our answer to the call to be one: "a gift we have been given" (Palmer 1998, 1).

The second consequence is that God invites us to be part of this trinitarian relationship. God invites us into this circle of love! This way we become *co-lovers* with God (Galatians 4:4-7).[1] As Torrance says: "God draws near to us in such a way as to draw near to himself within the circle of his knowing of himself" (Johnson 2002, 60). God does not invite us because He needs us. Since the love of the Lover and of the Loved One cannot be contained, God created us to be Co-lovers with Him. "God expands the circle to include us mere mortals, within the circle of his knowing of himself" (Johnson 2002, 63). Becoming co-lovers with God leads us to a relationship of worship towards God, to a relationship with each other, and with the world (John 15).

FOOD FOR THOUGHT

- What other images of community do we find in the Bible?
- What characteristics can you draw from them?

### ***The need for connexion***

> The silent churning at the core of our being is the tormenting need to know and to be known, to understand and to be understood, to possess and to be possessed, to belong unconditionally and forever without fear of loss, betrayal, or rejection. It is the nostalgia for our primal oneness, the silent sorrowing for embrace

[1] The term *co-lovers* is used by Scotus in James B. Torrance's *Worship, Community and the Triune God of Grace* (Carlisle: Paternoster Press, 1996), p. 72, and quoted by Darrell Johnson, *Experiencing the Trinity,* p. 62.

> of which we know we were created. It is the search, however wanton and sullied, for the pristine grace of holding and being held, for the freedom to be who we really are without shame or pretense, for release and response in the womb-like safety of unalterable acceptance and of overarching love. (Bilezikian 1997, 15)

Human beings have an innate desire for connexion that is etched into their DNA. Community, as God designed it, was only guaranteed success as long as its members were harmoniously connected to Him. This connexion with God was also what guaranteed the union with one another, thus covering the need for belonging. However, sin caused a disconnect not only between man and God, but also with himself and with his neighbour. The most tragic result of this event has been the continual dissatisfaction of not belonging, with all the consequences that arise from this.

The good news of the Gospel is good because, in Jesus, we have a new opportunity to reconnect with God and, consequently, with ourselves and with each other. "With atonement there is forgiveness, with forgiveness there is connection, and with connection there is the community of faith, a community destined to enter the bliss of perfect connection for ever" (Crabb 1997, 46). The family of faith becomes an opportunity for new hope of being part of something: being loved, belonging, respected, valued. "The Gospel bound believers to one another as well as to God [...] The Gospel is not a purely personal matter. It has a social dimension. It is a communal affair [...] To embrace the Gospel, then, it is to enter into community" (Banks 1999, 26-27). Responding to God's command to love each other as He loved us (John 12:34) allows the community to become a place in which love flows between the members. And, although it is true that this love must be a reflection of the love that comes from the triune God, the invitation is to love "[n]ot as much as he loves, but with him as he loves you. That is, I am to see him loving you and join him in his loving you" (Johnson 2002, 68). From this point of view, a community of love actually seems possible!

The new community in Christ goes far beyond living in harmony and enjoying the gift of belonging. It also provides the key means to fulfil God's purpose, not just for each member individually but especially for the community as a whole: the maturity of our faith, the transformation of our lives to the whole measure of the fullness of Christ (Ephesians 4:13):

> When people connect with each other on the basis of a vision for who they are and what they could become; when we see in others what little of Jesus has already begun to form beneath the insecurity, fear, and pride; when we long beyond anything else to see that little bit of Jesus develop and mature; then something is released from within us that has the power to form more of Jesus with them. (Crabb 1997, 65)

## Communities of learning

This brief reflection on biblical community should help us become aware of its importance. If community is a key instrument that God uses to transform us until we become like Jesus, then the indisputable context for formation for transformation should be the community of learning. Consequently, debates that call into question the validity of this form of learning are futile because it stems directly from God's design. Delving into the concept and purposes of Christian community is, therefore, a wake-up call for our way of understanding and carrying out training, which is normally characterised by individualism, competitiveness, success, personal interests, and personal development, to name just a few features. Talking about the community of learning does not mean merely reducing it to group techniques: "Simple changes in method will not accommodate the complex nature of learning and the facilitation of learning in community" (Cannell 2006, 301). As Cannell would say, we must go beyond the "cosmetic" (Cannell 2006, 301). So, what are the implications of this biblical model for the community of learning?

The community of learning is a beyond encouraging alternative that responds to the constant trend of reducing the teaching-learning process to a simple transmission of information, a trend we have already discussed in previous chapters. Palmer could not have expressed it better:

> These profound human transactions called knowing, teaching, and learning—are not just about information, and they're not just about getting jobs. They are about healing. They are about wholeness. They are about empowerment, liberation,

> transcendence. They are about reclaiming the vitality of life. (Palmer 1997, 3)

All these attributes are possible precisely within the context of community. This way of understanding education drives away, as Palmer puts it, the biggest enemy of learning: fear (Palmer 1993). For this, he explains, the key is to understand teaching differently: "To teach is to create a space in which the community of truth is practised" (Palmer 1993, XII).

### *Hospitality: creating the space to learn in community*

Aside from technical terms, methods, and invigorating programmes for group teaching – which can sometimes be superficial or even artificial – we must ask ourselves what it means to "create space". I would like to suggest and explore the important concept from Christian tradition that is hospitality, as a means that encourages the building of healthy Christian communities and, therefore, real communities of learning. Broadly speaking, Call defines hospitality as follows: "The physical manifestation of welcome – the welcoming spirit is demonstrated through specific actions [...] meant to facilitate comfort and care" (Smith 2001, 64). Nouwen goes further and, thinking about the effect of the fall on our relationships with each other, says: "Primarily the creation of a free space where the stranger can enter and become a friend instead of an enemy" (Nouwen 1998, 49).

### FOOD FOR THOUGHT

- What does the idea of the student as a "stranger" suggest to you?

Applying hospitality to the educational context leads us to the following challenge, which Marmon frames well: "What would be different about your teaching if you thought of yourself as a host and of your students as guests?" (Marmon 2008, 34). Next, we should also ask ourselves: Is the role of host exclusive to the teacher and the role of guest exclusive to the student? Or are we all, in one way or another, hosts and guests? Even more importantly: What does being good hosts and good guests represent? These are some of the questions we will analyse in the following sections.

## Food for Thought

- Create a list of the characteristics of a good host and of a good guest.
- How can the teacher be a guest at the same time as a host?
- How can the student be a host at the same time as a guest?

### *The characteristics of hospitality in an educational context*

> Teaching [...] asks first of all for the creation of a space where students and teachers can enter into a fearless communication with each other and allow their respective life experiences to be their primary and most valuable source of growth and maturation. It asks for a mutual trust in which those who teach and those who want to learn can become present to each other, not as opponents, but as those who share in the same struggle and search for the same truth. (Nouwen 1998, 60)

If hospitality "is not something you do as much as it is someone you become" (Smith 2001, 78), then instead of techniques, we should aim for character formation and adopting values that point towards real transformation. This means that, first, a community of learning that flows from divine love and that has relational capacity will naturally, and primarily, be based on respectful relationships. Each member of the community honours their classmate as someone who has intrinsic value because their value comes from the Creator, who recognises them as His child and loves them. This is why each member also deserves my love and consideration. In turn, that respect becomes reverence towards God, an act of worship, a pleasing offering.

Respectful relationships are reflected in the classroom not only through a store of mutual trust but also through a commitment to that trust solidifying and growing. Trust allows us to accept and not see other people's vision and contribution as a threat, as something suspicious, or even as something that should be rejected from the start, but rather as a different point of view which broadens my way of seeing things and enriches my life. After all, life cannot be seen from only one perspective. "Knowing and learning are communal acts. They require many eyes and ears, many observations and experiences. They require a continual cycle of discussion, disagreement, and consensus over what has been seen and what it all means" (Palmer, 6). What's more, when relationships are respectful, they cause one to be open towards others, which allows me to be a giver, but also to become a receiver. This attitude shows humility, an attitude that confirms that I am not above others and that I don't use the power I have at my disposal. It is a sign that I put myself at the same level, that I submit to walking with others along the same path because I believe that walking with them makes us stronger and wiser. In short, we deeply believe that when we learn together, we learn better.

Second, the community of learning is based on what Palmer has coined as "creative conflict", a concept that he defines as, "public encounter in which the whole group can win by growing" (Palmer, 7). Creative conflict is what allows a community to confront itself in a healthy way and with the aim of growing. Conflict that is understood this way is diametrically opposed to the individual competitiveness that eats away at our society nowadays, even in any educational institution or activity and even in the Church. Conflict, which can often be triggered by fear – fear of incompetence, of not measuring up, of not belonging, of ignorance – can be redeemed within the context of a community of love and compassion that looks after each other (Palmer, 7). We must get rid of the idea that failure is something to be avoided, passed over or hidden, something to feel guilty or even ashamed about. Once we get up again, failure is what allows us to see things differently and influence with a better knowledge of the facts and more humility. It is actually what allows us to grow and change. When we give ourselves space to fail, we give ourselves space to experiment, learn, conquer our fears and, as a matter of fact, limit the possibility of error in the future. It opens up a door for us to look for the other person and collaborate, mutually benefiting from our gifts, knowledge, and experiences. More importantly, failure reveals our weaknesses and limitations – which we have actually been created with! And that leads to us depending less upon ourselves and more on God, in a dependent relationship, and depending more on each other, in an interdependent relationship.

FOOD FOR THOUGHT

- Consider the challenging situations when you teach and the "ungrateful" students you come across. How could you practise hospitality?
- In these contexts, what does it mean to give one's life and demonstrate love?

## Encouraging community among teachers: positioning ourselves as a community

Up until now, we have talked about community as a space for encouraging the teaching-learning process. Although we will discuss at length the importance of self-care for teachers in chapter 9, in order to have a lasting ministry, I think that as we end this chapter it is appropriate to discuss the importance of also creating spaces of mutual support among teachers. If, as teachers, we want to be community builders, then we must also embody this reality among ourselves as a teaching body. Our most immediate community is our own community of teachers, defined in the same way we have defined it so far. What are the ingredients for this community of teachers?

First, a community of teachers looks after each other. Actually, mutual care is in accordance with the very design of God: the body of Christ. The apostle Paul uses this beautiful illustration when he refers to the people of God: "Now you are the body of Christ, and each one of you is a part of it" (1 Corinthians 12:27). It explains the importance of fraternal love, despite our differences, and how these differences actually complement us and mutually build us up. Being connected with each other is an opportunity that has an eternal impact of spiritual transformation which goes far beyond simply fulfilling a series of functional duties.

Leaders should oversee the building of collaborative teams of teachers and they should avoid favouritism, which easily provokes quarrels, jealousy, conflict, and competitiveness. This implies taking intentional steps towards mutual care and support: communities that provide safe spaces where teachers feel protected, accepted, and where they know they belong. They are communities who know how to combine genuine communication and love. Not only do they provide material care, but they are first and foremost a place where people can minister to and pray for one another. These communities are characterised by open communication, conflict resolution, pastoral care, and prayer (Hardy, 2012). When these types of communities are built, they become a platform for learning together and, consequently, growing and maturing together.

Second, in a community of teachers, everyone holds each other accountable. When teachers commit to encouraging each other along their path, that commitment acts as a guarantee. Mentors, spiritual directors, and others can be very positive influences in this process because they "raise the level of our energy to do God's will" (McDonald 2007, 66). We will discuss this in more depth in chapter 8 when we talk about sustainable teaching.

Finally, a community of teachers makes room for creativity. A lack of creativity can cause all sorts of tensions in the life of an institution. It is vital to make room for wonder and amazement because these values nurture creativity. We create because we are the Creator's creation. "In creativity our actions link up to the creative work of the universe" (Fox 1985, 49). When we create, we are closer to God. When we create, we position ourselves to regularly be spiritually renewed. Leaders must make sure they give their teachers the space they need for creativity and do not just expect them to yield and produce, to respond to skills and curricula, and to present exam results.

When we provide support structures for teachers, they will not be the only beneficiaries. Students will also benefit because "[i]t is in the character of the teacher that will largely influence what kind of student outcome we can expect" (Issler 1996, 215). In the end, we will see entire institutions and societies renewed.

## Conclusion

As teachers, we are primarily responsible for not only adopting the biblical concept of community of learning in our teaching, but also for building these communities. We mainly do this through offering up our own lives and daily showing our love for teaching as well as our love for the students.

Cannell challenges us, saying: "Think first of the church as the people of God, rather than as an organization defined by programs. Then envision those experiences that are necessary for the maturing and spiritual development of the entire congregation" (Cannell 2006, 259). If our ministries revolve around people, how do we tackle the need to plan our training so that it is not only long-lasting but also sustainable? This will be the subject of the following chapter.

# Chapter 8

## A Sustainable Teaching Ministry

> While you live, you learn; and while you learn, you live. (Hendricks 2003, 18)

In the Bible, concepts such as being a disciple, maturing, and learning are not finite processes. Knowing Jesus intimately means knowing who He is and what He asks of us, and the consequence of that is that we are obedient with our lives, by submitting our whole being to Christ: our mind, our heart, our emotions, and our attitudes.

In his letter to the Philippians, Paul writes:

> Brothers and sisters, I do not consider myself yet to have taken hold of it. But one thing I do: Forgetting what is behind and straining toward what is ahead, I press on toward the goal to win the prize for which God has called me heavenward in Christ Jesus. (Philippians 3:13-14)

The apostle is exhorting his brothers and sisters in Philippi to stand firm in their faith, warning them of the dangers that can take away their joy. He earnestly shares his testimony with them: he considers the past to be rubbish – what is crucial is the future. His insistence on repeating that he has not yet reached the goal does not suggest he is disheartened, rather it shows his eagerness to reach the desired objective.

More often than we would like to admit, when we know we need to persevere, our natural response is to become discouraged; after all, our culture is all about "fast" and "low cost", and we are not prepared or willing to take on long processes that are (often) tedious, painful, and sacrificial. However, the reasons for being encouraged that we can infer from this passage by far outstrip the disadvantages. First, God invites us to work with what we know, not with what we do not know. But, He also has so much more in store for us! And this should be motivation enough for us to have an open and teachable attitude, so that we can continue to be instructed, convicted, guided, challenged, and rebuked, precisely because we learn to be aware of the fact that we have not yet reached this attitude.

Second, God invites us to consider our walk and our transformation into the image of Christ as a lifelong process, not as a one-time event. Circumstances, relationships, crises, and victories, which can sometimes feel like obstacles, are actually part of God's strategy to carry out His work in us, in His time and in His perfect way. We can get up every day, experiencing peace and encouragement to carry on because His mercies are new every morning (Lamentations 3:22-23); "We are hard pressed on every side, but not crushed; perplexed, but not in despair; persecuted, but not abandoned; struck down, but not destroyed" (2 Corinthians 4:8-9). No circumstance in life, no matter how negative it is, has the power of the last word. In His grace, "we all, [...] are being transformed into his image *with ever-increasing glory*, which comes from the Lord, who is the Spirit" (2 Corinthians 3:18, emphasis added).

If our transformative journey is one that lasts a lifetime, then this should also apply to training. In this chapter we want to explore, first, what ongoing learning implies and, second, the importance of training others with the aim of having sustainable ministries. We will end by discussing the need for evaluation within our educational contexts.

FOOD FOR THOUGHT

- How do you know whether you are moving forward in your walk with Christ?
- How do you assess your spiritual health?

## Ongoing learning

In Paul's message to the Philippians, both the verb and the verb tense are significant. "Press on" not only conveys that he has not yet reached the desired place, but it also emphasises the action of persisting with an unfinished action. Paul must continue doing what he was already doing:

gaining Christ. When we apply this idea to the context of training, the most relevant principle we can deduce is that we cannot merely link training to a programme, nor can we reduce it to an event. However, if we carry out an honest assessment of the way we develop training in our ministry contexts, it turns out that this is what happens time and again. For example, we encounter churches that painstakingly work on their Sunday school programmes for children's training. But, once these children reach a certain age (sometimes only 12 or 13 years old), they must move on to the adult service without any kind of follow-up. The most tragic consequence is that many teenagers simply stop going to church because there has been no guidance to help them understand how it is relevant to their lives.

We see parachurch organisations that plan and offer events into which large amounts of time, human resources, and materials are poured. These events chiefly revolve around a good programme with well-known speakers who present large amounts of information. Participants are simply consumerist receptors, and although they might make the effort to take notes in their beautifully designed notebooks, these will just end up on a shelf and never be opened again. Evaluation forms are handed out, but either no one takes the time to go through them when the time comes to plan the next event, or they are not taken seriously enough to question how we do things. There are also well-intentioned churches that organise training seminars that do not actually respond to the real needs and concerns of their members, or during which they teach things members already know, without asking for their opinion or contribution.

## Food for Thought

- Consider the training you have access to, have had access to, or even the one you are planning. Is it primarily based on an event? Why? Describe it.

One of the ways in which we can treat formation as a process in our ministry contexts is to stop thinking "let's invite this person to an event" and think instead "let's invite this person on a journey of transformation". The responsibility of leaders when it comes to the spiritual formation of their members should not be reduced to a precise moment in their lives, rather it should span every one of a person's natural stages of development, from when they are born until the Lord calls them to His presence. If our training proposals are primarily marked by "event culture", how can we transform them in order to build a culture of "ongoing learning"? How can we get the most out of specific events within the process of learning?

### FOOD FOR THOUGHT

- Think about the events that you organise or attend. What impact has the event had over time, once it was over?
- How could this impact be improved?
- How could the duration of the impact be increased?

First, we must come up with event proposals that do not focus on packing in as much information as possible. We should pay attention to the content, but also to the pedagogy. For example, listening to an expert is only one way of learning and the reality is that most of what we learn does not come from "the pulpit". We can offer a variety of spaces that encourage different ways of learning. In fact, these spaces often occur naturally without the need for organisational intervention, such as the numerous conversations that happen around the meal table. As a matter of fact, this should lead us to promote these spaces, recognising them and enhancing them in order to maximise learning. We could lighten the moments that offer content and give more free time, or encourage opportunities for exchange among equals.

Although it is biblical to recognise that God bestows the gift of teaching on some people in particular, as we have already discussed and highlighted in chapter 7, we must remember that everybody learns from everybody, together, in communities of learning. Events bring together many people who are open to receiving, but who also have a lot to give, and who want to give. What's more, our culture values the idea that everyone has room to contribute! The excessive emphasis on the need to have so-called experts can be misleading, as well as leading us into idolatry and disregarding or ignoring other people's potential. On the one hand, this inevitably leads to a comfortable culture in which the receiver simply expects to receive. This attitude easily leads to spiritual laziness, to a demanding consumerist attitude and, worst of all, to our hearts becoming numb. And, on the other hand, the truth is that we often choose the "experts" according to their reputation or because they are people who know things but who do not necessarily know how to communicate in such a way that those who are listening learn and are transformed. Maybe this should lead us to redefine the profile of the speaker we invite to our events, whether it be a workshop, seminar, or plenary.

## EXERCISE

**Speaker profile**

In light of what we have presented so far, imagine you are preparing an event:

· Who are the participants?

· What are their needs?

· What are the various learning spaces?

· With all this in mind, what profile should the speaker you want to invite have? Write it out as if it were an official document describing a job.

Second, we should think about how we design processes that could help people before and after the event. In other words, how do we want them to prepare for the event and how will we help them implement what they have learned afterwards? As a general rule, we pour all our effort and preparation into our content. We ask ourselves what people need to know, usually based on our assumptions rather than based on real needs and context, as we mentioned in chapter 6. Undoubtedly, content is important, but we must also ask ourselves what we want people to become, because we want to see people completely transformed. Therefore, it would be good if we considered, for example, what attitudes we want to promote before, during, and after the event. These attitudes may include a willingness to give and the humility to receive, which are very different to a consumerist attitude. Additionally, a willingness to learn, and to do so in different ways, which stands in contrast to the prideful attitude of thinking we know everything. In order to truly learn, an explicit willingness to obey by implementing what was learned is also important. That is without a doubt the number one reason why we often cannot learn: we don't want to obey! Our aim should be for people to have an individual and unselfish receiving attitude, being aware of the fact that they are part of a community. That is why we try to encourage them to reflect on how what they have received can be beneficial for the churches and ministries they are part of because, at the end of the day, our calling is to be the Church.

## Food for Thought

- When you participate in or prepare a training event, what are your personal objectives? What do you want for your life?
- When you participate in or prepare a training event, what are your group objectives? What do you want for the people you are training?

When we keep these suggestions in mind and understand that learning should start before the event, take shape during the event, and continue afterwards – that is, when the event is not the focus of the training but part of the training process – then we will realise that the event has become part of a process and it will be much easier to implement the necessary changes. Among other things, this will help us network, as we seek to connect our events with others within the organisation and/or denomination and find ways to maximise the events via virtual platforms.

## Notes for Leaders

**Ongoing learning for teachers**

Ongoing learning doesn't just benefit the people we serve – it also benefits teachers. In order to implement these paradigm shifts we have suggested, there are two key aspects that need to be worked on:

> First, teachers need to be empowered to help students be accountable for their own learning journey. It is a collaboration, in which they become responsible for instructing, motivating, and guiding students in their learning process.
>
> Second, teachers need to be equipped to adopt a facilitating role instead of perpetuating the model of the teacher as the only one who holds and can transmit the truth. This requires a learning community of teachers who make themselves vulnerable and show that they are open to learning from students. It is also necessary for them to have the support and space they need for their spiritual development, as we will discuss in more depth in chapter 9.

Ongoing learning doesn't just benefit the people we serve – it also benefits teachers. In order to implement these paradigm shifts we have suggested, there are two key aspects that need to be worked on:

First, teachers need to be empowered to help students be accountable for their own learning journey. It is a collaboration, in which they become responsible for instructing, motivating, and guiding students in their learning process.

Second, teachers need to be equipped to adopt a facilitating role instead of perpetuating the model of the teacher as the only one who holds and can transmit the truth. This requires a learning community of teachers who make themselves vulnerable and show that they are open to learning from students. It is also necessary for them to have the support and space they need for their spiritual development, as we will discuss in more depth in chapter 9.

Sometimes, the things we know best are the ones we put into practice the least. It is a sad reality! And yet, this is precisely one of the reasons why God gives us the opportunity to learn through a long process that lasts a lifetime. One example of this is the well-known passage often referred to as the Great Commission, but which has also been referred to as "the great omission", to reflect how it has been interpreted and used wrongly:

> Therefore, go and make disciples of all nations, baptising them in the name of the Father and of the Son and of the Holy Spirit, and teaching them to obey everything I have commanded you. And surely, I am with you always, to the very end of the age. (Matthew 28:19-20)

The use of the gerund, "teaching", expresses a lasting action, which reminds us that teaching occurs over a period of time. Another example of a wrong interpretation: this passage is used to emphasise preaching the gospel and making converts, whereas the call is actually to make disciples. If we want to talk about sustainable ministries, we forcibly have to talk about how we involve others and how we prepare them. This is the following topic we will discuss in this chapter.

## A model for multiplication

People have always been key to God's work because He wants to use us for His purposes. We see this from the very beginning, when He established His people, the people of Israel. And we continue to see it, not only in the way Jesus developed His own ministry, but in the type of ministry He established for His disciples and, consequently, for His

Church. From a human perspective, Jesus' methods may seem shocking. After all, isn't He God? Doesn't that identity make Him capable of developing a ministry based on His own efforts, without the help of human beings? In the Bible, we read that Jesus "made himself nothing by taking the very nature of a servant, being made in human likeness" (Philippians 2:7), and in fact, that earned the Father's approval, before He even started His ministry (Matthew 3:17)! The main reason why Jesus willingly and strategically took on this ministry format derives from His very essence: God is triune and Jesus' model of ministry reflects the Trinity, as we mentioned in chapter 7.

What's more, Jesus knew beforehand that His time on earth was limited and that, if He wanted to see His work carried on, He had to prepare others. Moreover, Jesus was also aware of the limitations that stemmed from His humanity: He needed rest because He tired of the various demands of ministry, He needed to eat and drink, He was geographically limited because He could not be everywhere at once, and He depended on His Father and submitted to Him.

The way in which Jesus did ministry is a realistic model for us because we also have limitations that, however hard we try, we cannot avoid (even though we ignore them all too often and that leads to multiple ministerial crises). First, what I mean by realistic is that it is possible, because when we don't work alone, we can reach more places and the Kingdom spreads significantly. Additionally, we honour all the people who make up the body of Christ, with their callings and gifts, as we highlighted in chapter 7. Second, it is sustainable, because ministry should not depend on us. Although we are part of God's plan and He equips and trains us to fulfil his purposes, we are not indispensable. Jesus invites us to share our load (Matthew 11:28-30) and Paul reminds us that we can and should share it with others (Galatians 6:2-4).

All too often, instead of being an opportunity to practise our callings and gifts, our ministries are platforms that feed our egos. Instead of an opportunity to serve, they are an excuse to manipulate others in order to fulfil our own purposes. We acquire titles and ministry posts, and we ensconce ourselves so that no one can get rid of us. Our churches and organisations are led by the same people who either settle into a role without a finite contract and without clear-cut review protocols until it gets to the point that no one dares say anything, or they take turns in one role or another, never leaving room for new faces and a breath of fresh air. Not only do these attitudes make it difficult for there to be change and renewal, but they also lead to excesses that, in time, lead to exhaustion, which then leads to ministries coming to a forced standstill – sometimes only for a time, sometimes indefinitely. Other consequences include crises of faith and vocation, family breakdowns brought on by integrity slip-ups, absence, and negligence. The most tragic reality is that our ministries lack power and do not bear fruit. Ultimately, they do not reflect the glory God deserves and the salt that should flavour our broken world is so insipid that it has the opposite effect.

When we say we are going to train others, we are taking on the commitment of passing on the baton, and the way in which we do it will reveal whether our identity is found in ourselves or in Christ.

Paul appeals to Timothy, saying: "And the things you have heard me say in the presence of many witnesses entrust to reliable people who will also be qualified to teach others" (2 Timothy 2:2). By committing to training other teachers so that they can develop their own vocation, their calling from God, and their gifts, and so that they will take over when the opportune moment presents itself, we demonstrate that we have understood our ministry as one that multiplies. We demonstrate that we really love people because God loved us first.

## Food for Thought

- Who is your Paul?
- Who is your Timothy?
- How do you make sure that you are passing on the baton?
- How do you care for other people's ongoing learning and care?

The process of training others has to do with looking for, recognising, and developing other people's gifts; offering opportunities to those who are younger or less experienced; walking alongside them as they experiment and develop their vocation and gifts; offering constructive feedback in order to evaluate how they are growing. This is an area we will explore in more detail in the following sections.

**Identifying, training, developing, and caring for future teachers**

**1. Recruitment**

a. Why do we need more teachers and what for?
b. What do we look for in prospective teachers?
c. How do we select them?

**2. Job descriptions and teacher development**

a. How do we establish the profile of a teacher?
b. How do we write job descriptions? What should they include?
c. Do we invite potential candidates to write their own job descriptions?
d. How often should the job descriptions be re-evaluated?
e. How do we share the vision and help teachers stay passionate about their ministries?
f. How do we help teachers go above and beyond their responsibilities and tasks?
g. How do we establish realistic development goals?
h. How do we avoid burnout and early departures?
i. How can we help teachers end well?

**3. Training**

a. How do we understand training teachers? Why is it important?
b. Is systematic training necessary? How worthwhile is it?
c. What place do formal and informal training have?
d. How do we identify training needs? What are areas teachers need to be trained in? How do we design curricula?

e. How can we design curricula so that they reflect the diversity and distinct characters of each teacher and their specific situations?
f. Do we train teachers to be able to train others?
g. How does the training methodology influence a teacher's development? Do we inform or do we seek transformation? How is this evident in our training?
h. How do we appreciate and make the most of opportunities for training outside of our organisation?

**4. Training a support team**

a. How do we encourage team building among our teachers?
b. How do we help them support, appreciate, and complement each other?
c. How often is it good and necessary to meet?
d. What are the best "spaces" to meet in?
e. How do we involve others in helping our teachers?
f. How do we support the teacher's family?

**5. Supervision and communication**

a. What does it mean to supervise? What should supervision include?
b. How do we set realistic supervision goals? How do we arrive at a consensus so that expectations are met?
c. How can we ensure that our supervision also includes pastoral care? In what practical ways can we look after teachers?
d. How often should supervisory meetings take place?
e. How often should assessments be carried out?

## Assessment

FOOD FOR THOUGHT

- Consider some of the difficulties you have experienced or are experiencing when you teach. Write them down.
- Decide what area they belong to: student, teacher, programme/resource.
- How have you resolved these difficulties?

How do we know our students are learning? Moreover, how can we assess whether our students have changed and how they have changed? How can we train others, providing feedback in safe and constructive spaces? How do we assess our own growth? As we saw in chapter 1, evaluating people's spiritual formation is no easy task. Maybe this is the reason why we don't have evaluation procedures (or if we do, they are unsatisfactory). Sometimes it is because our learning goals lack evaluation parameters or because the focus is on quantitative assessment on the academic side because of academic pressure. At the end of the day, this can lead us to question whether spiritual formation can even be evaluated!

FOOD FOR THOUGHT

- How do you assess growth among the people you serve?
- How do you evaluate your own growth – both personal and within ministry?

First, we should ask ourselves: "Why is assessment important?". Assessment – and in this case we are referring to ongoing assessment – benefits students because it enables us to correct learning or a mistake/misunderstanding, appreciate present achievements, and predict future learning capabilities. It also helps teachers monitor their teaching rhythm and evaluate the curriculum. Furthermore, assessments benefit the institution by reporting present achievement, estimating aptitude for new learning and potential for responsibility, and providing a character reference (Harkness 1989, 188).

### Food for Thought

- How often do you sit in on a colleague's class or vice versa?
- Has a colleague ever assessed your teaching or vice versa?
- How could you introduce assessment among colleagues?
- Is there anything you feel reluctant about?

Second, what are we supposed to measure? Harkness proposes four parameters for assessment, which offer an integral vision of the learning process: "cognitive acquisition of appropriate knowledge, competence in required ministerial/pastoral skills, personal character development and empathy and compassion" (Harkness 2008, 94).

## ADDITIONAL RESOURCES

**Summative and formative assessment**

In a learning-centred approach the most common forms are the summative and formative assessments. Summative assessment "tries to summarize student learning at some point in time" (Kennedy, Hyland and Ryan 2012, 21), usually at the end of a course, and can be defined as "a measure of what has been achieved [...] It is often expressed as a numerical number or grade" (Cheesman 2009, 1).

Formative assessment is "assessment for learning" (Kennedy, Hyland and Ryan 2012, 20), "an estimate of achievement in process in order to help the learning process which is provisional, complicated and lays the emphasis on advice" (Cheesman 2009, 2). Both are important and needed because the grade in the summative assessment has ceased to be the only valid form of assessment, as it often does not do justice to the overall learning of the student and their formative process.

Third, who do we measure? What seems obvious and what often happens is that teachers evaluate students. But we should also implement feedback among colleagues; students should assess teachers and their courses; and there should be institutional assessment, assessment among colleagues, and self-assessment. "The eliciting effect occurs when, through modelling, the teacher teaches the art of giving and receiving feedback by inviting the learners to constructively criticize his or her own performance" (Knowles, Holton and Swanson 2005, 103). Even so, we must go beyond implementing assessment processes. We must create "a culture of feedback": open and safe spaces, based on trust, in which people are free to give and receive feedback.

Perhaps we should reflect on whether the reason why we don't assess students is because we are not willing to assess ourselves or let others assess us, and therefore we cannot do it with integrity. Although it is true that this requires a high degree of vulnerability, there is too much at stake if we do not carry out these assessments. Instead of seeing it as a threat, we could see it as a tool that not only helps us improve our abilities but also helps us grow and mature in Christ.

## NOTE FOR LEADERS

We can ease some of the reluctance by taking into account and looking for ways to alleviate the other pressures teachers are exposed to. These pressures reduce the attention they should also be giving to spiritual formation and practical ministry training.

## ADDITIONAL RESOURCES

**Feedback in teaching**

Feedback involves giving some objective information about a person's behaviour and the way it affects others. It must be clearly distinguished from praise and criticism [...] Feedback [...] is meant to encourage a thinking response, as distinct from an emotional one.

- Describe attitudes and actions.
- Describe the effects of these attitudes and actions on others.
- As part of the feedback, check your own perceptions of what happened.
- Be specific. Describe feelings.

(Baumohl 1987, 147)

## EXERCISE

Choose one of the following activities:

1. Ask another teacher, a colleague, or a friend to observe one of your classes and give you feedback.

2. Ask a student to anonymously fill out this short questionnaire. Phrase the questions to receive feedback, such as:
   - What do you find appealing about our class?
   - What characteristics of the teacher's personality help or distract?
   - What do you find boring about our class?
   - If you could change one thing about our class, what would it be?

3. Record one of your classes (video or audio) and write down two things that could be improved.

4. Observe another professor. Write down one or two things you have learned from them and make a plan of how to incorporate some of them.

## Conclusion

Jesus himself lived out and developed a ministry that had its limits in order to show us a sustainable model. We must project our training into the future because our race is not over until we reach glory. On the other hand, we should not run alone. We must embrace the idea that part of our ministry is to invest in training others who are prepared to take up the baton.

However, a long-term race – which we run intentionally, depending on the Holy Spirit, open to examining and assessing, and devoted to the students – must be accompanied by self-care. As teachers, our number one priority must be our own spiritual health. This will be the subject of the following chapter.

# Chapter 9

## A Teacher's Own Development

> A capable teacher is "far more precious than jewels". He works diligently, plans wisely, and uses resources carefully. She reaches out to others, cares well for herself and those in charge, and lives a life of dignity and kindness. We entrust our children, youth, and adults to the ministrations of our teachers and rely on those teachers to help pass along what we Christians claim is the most important story in our lives. Teachers are in the business of helping God to form, inform, and transform persons to have within themselves the mind of Christ and to love out of that love and commitment. They deserve all the love, support, and respect we can offer. We owe it to them to "praise their work in the city gates. (Paraphrase of Proverbs 31:10-31; Hynson 2006, 6-8)

As teachers, we are called to give ourselves to students, so logically it follows that we must also look after ourselves. If we intend to redeem spirituality in teaching, then it must also be our priority as teachers: we should not only aim to fulfil our professional duties, but above all, we should also aim to develop ourselves and stay spiritually refreshed. Consequently, this implies a constant movement of spiritual renewal.

### Spirituality in teaching

In this chapter we want to propose that, as teachers, we are invited to not only consider what we will call our "professional" development – strategies, techniques, and skills – but also our personal development, and especially our spiritual development. In fact, spiritual and personal development are real needs that, once satisfied, open the door to working on professional needs. Intrator and Kunzman explain that we should start with "the soul of the enterprise, the passion and purpose that animate teacher's ongoing commitment to students and learning" (Intrator and Kunzman 2006, 38-42); and Palmer adds that we should seek the "integral health" of teachers and help them "not to live divided" (Palmer 1998, 64, 167). This leads us to the question: What does it mean to cultivate our spirit so that it directly influences the spirit of our teaching? We want to look far beyond programmes, methodologies, or bodies of knowledge. We want to go beyond doing and focus on being. This opens the way to something deeper, something that has more to do with shaping our character and the transformation of our heart. As Issler puts it: "It is the character of the teacher that will largely influence what kind of student outcome we can expect" because "teaching […] involves a life influencing a life" (Issler 1996, 215, 216).

### *Guidelines for spiritual development*

What are the key elements of a spirituality that keeps us alive as teachers? First, we must reflect the Trinity. Its three members are clear examples that we can learn from. We can imitate God: "Every time the Lord reveals Himself to us, He is teaching. Therefore, God, by His very nature, is a teacher" (Esqueda 2008, 34). Likewise, we can imitate the Teacher of teachers, Jesus. He reached everyone, He showed compassion, He understood His audience and He mastered the Scriptures. When He taught, says Esqueda, "Jesus was more interested in internal character than external *show*" (Esqueda 2008, 65), which makes His teachings about more than merely transmitting information. These were an opportunity for true character formation. The role of the Holy Spirit is also essential for any impact on people's hearts, as we looked at in chapter 3. Esqueda says: "The Holy Spirit helps Christian teachers by giving them discernment of God's truths and empowering them to instruct students in a way that produces spiritual transformation" (Esqueda 2008, 76). When we imitate the Trinity and cultivate our souls, we become reflective mirrors, models for the lives of those we teach. Not only is the Trinity our model agent, but also the agent we partner with for spiritual growth.

Second, we must become true disciples of Jesus. Pazmiño says that: "Christian spirituality for teachers implies a discipleship centered upon Jesus Christ as Lord and a walk with Christ's Spirit, the Holy Spirit" (Pazmiño 1994, 144). A disciple is recognised by their fruit: "Thus, by their fruit you will recognise them" (Matthew 7:20). Therefore, a disciple is not only someone who follows their master and wants to do what he does, but also wants to be like him. When we follow Jesus, we can see how He obeys the Father: "Very truly I tell you, the Son can do nothing by himself; he can do only what he sees his Father doing, because whatever the Father does the Son also does" (John 5:19). Discipleship is not a static state one enters and remains in; nor is it a state that applies to our spirituality. It implies growth. Paul's appeal to Timothy may illuminate our discussion:

> Command and teach these things. Don't let anyone look down on you because you are young, but set an example for the believers in speech, in conduct, in love, in faith and in purity. Until I come, devote yourself to the public reading of Scripture, to preaching and to teaching. Do not neglect your gift, which was given you through prophecy when the body of elders laid their hands on you. Be diligent in these matters; give yourself wholly to them, so that everyone may see your progress. Watch your life and doctrine closely. Persevere in them, because if you do, you will save both yourself and your hearers. (1 Timothy 4:11-16)

Discipleship affects all aspects of life. It affects our entire being. For this reason, God is interested in every aspect of a teacher's life, and He therefore makes sure their growth is holistic. This is a lifelong process:

> A disciple is a lifelong learner [...] an intentional imitator [...] a spiritual apprentice [...] a lifelong pursuer of the real and only life [...] a forever student in the school of Jesus Christ [...] so that our thoughts, words, actions, and motives might gradually become more like his. (McDonald 2007, 46)

Third, we must pursue the transformation of our hearts. In Greek, the word for transformation is *metamorphoō* (μεταμορφόω) and it means "to change into another form" or "to transfigure". This word is used twice in the New Testament in the context of a believer's transformation. The first is in 2 Corinthians: "And we all, who with unveiled faces contemplate the Lord's glory, are being transformed into his image with ever-increasing glory, which comes from the Lord, who is the Spirit" (2 Corinthians 3:18). The second time appears in Romans, "Do not conform to the pattern of this world, but be transformed by the renewing of your mind. Then you will be able to test and approve what God's will is—his good, pleasing and perfect will" (Romans 12:2), a passage we studied in depth in chapter 2. In light of the present discussion, it is worth picking up the thread of the arguments we presented in that chapter. Grenz defines it as:

> The word metamorphoumetha, here rendered "we are being transformed", describes a change not just of outward form but of

> inner essence. Both the present tense of this verb and the words "from one degree of glory to another" (RSV) indicate that this transformation is not instantaneous but progressive. (Gundry 1987, 77)

This concept is in sharp contrast with the reductionist idea of a change of attitude or change of mind. It goes deeper and requires divine intervention because no real transformation can result from only the teacher's effort. Willard says emphatically:

> The renovation of the heart into Christlikeness – that is, in humanity as God always intended it – is not something that concerns the heart (Spirit, will) alone. The heart cannot be renovated if the other aspects of the person remain in the grip of evil. "Will-power" – is not the key to personal transformation. Rather, the will and character only progress in effectual well-being as all other essential aspects of the person come into line with the intent of a will brought to newness of life "from above" by the Word and the Spirit. (Willard 2002, 253)

Change is carried out by the transforming work and power of the Holy Spirit, in collaboration with an open attitude and the development of our self-awareness.

### *Guidelines for personal development*

As teachers, how do we develop ourselves personally? First, as we have already looked at previously, we must be sure to have a spiritual centre, sure that we are anchored in our relationship with Jesus, and that there is a continuous growth towards full maturity. We understand and live in a way that shows that our identity is hidden in Christ (Colossians 3:3). This means that we are not people who easily waver when faced with external circumstances: difficult disciples, organisational and structural challenges, power struggles with colleagues, etc.

Second, our vocation and values must be clear. Most teachers will assert that a sense of calling and vocation is precisely what motivates them to teach. In his letter to the Romans, the apostle Paul mentions that teaching is a free gift, distributed by the Spirit as He pleases, and if we have received it, he encourages us to use it: "We have different gifts, according to the grace given to each of us. If your gift [...] is teaching, then teach" (Romans 12:6-7). He also emphasises that these gifts have been given in the context of the body of Christ: "Now you are the body of Christ, and each one of you is a part of it. And God has placed in the church first of all apostles, second prophets, third teachers [...]" (1 Corinthians 12:27-28). And for the purpose of building up the body of Christ: "So Christ himself gave [...] teachers, to equip his people for works of service, so that the body of Christ may be built up" (Ephesians 4:11-12).

### Food for Thought

- Why do you teach?
- What motivates you to get up in the morning?
- Who is your teaching role model?
- What traits make you a great teacher?
- What situations make you doubt your own ability?
- What situations confirm that you were destined to teach?

(Dress 2012, 28-31)

At the same time, we must work for our values because when we do, we show integrity. Pazmiño says:

> For Christian teachers, the call is to seek to be and become all that they affirm in their teaching, thereby modelling a wholeness and integrity. This also requires of teachers the willingness to admit

> when their actions are not consistent with their stated or implied values. (Pazmiño 1998, 82)

This is even more crucial nowadays because, as Cain reminds us, there has been a serious deterioration of the value system. He suggests that it has led adults to fall "into a lack of vision so total that we can no longer live up to what we profess to believe" (Cain 2001, 702), and that they consequently need "to rediscover their values, [...] to believe in absolutes once more [...] without imposing it on others" (Cain 2001, 702). This is clearly in line with Paul's reasoning, who says that we should not conform to the pattern of this time, but that we should be transformed by the renewing of our minds (Romans 12:2), as we discussed in chapter 2.

Third, we should nurture in ourselves a sense of awe and amazement. "Learning", says Fox, "is as natural – and as necessary for survival – as eating or drinking. It should be just as delicious" (Fox 1985, 49). The Bible maintains there is a link between our amazement and our relationship with God: "The fear of the Lord is the beginning of wisdom, and knowledge of the Holy One is understanding" (Proverbs 9:10). In this context, fear is not synonymous with panic, anxiety, horror, doubt, or fear. It has to do with recognising the majesty and greatness of the Lord and the fact that He is God, and we are not. This is why He should be revered. When we can see beyond what the people we teach are doing, and we can instead reflect on what they are experiencing in the process, we nurture our sense of wonder. The reference point is not limited to what I as a teacher can teach or communicate but resides specifically in seeing how students learn. On the practical side, we can write down these experiences, in diary form for example, and even share them afterwards. However small these stories may be, they are true windows of hope when it seems that nothing is happening. Our memory constantly needs to be refreshed.

Wonder and awe are often rekindled by gratitude. The psalmist exhorts us time and time again to always give thanks: "Many, Lord my God, are the wonders you have done, the things you planned for us. None can compare with you; were I to speak and tell of your deeds, they would be too many to declare" (Psalm 40:5). And the apostle Paul does the same thing by leading us to believe that gratitude should be an act of obedience within the context of our loving relationship with the Lord: "Give thanks in all circumstances; for this is God's will for you in Christ Jesus" (1 Thessalonians 5:8). Fox adds that gratitude is part of our process of maturity: "Appreciation is an attitude we take with us through life. When we grow in gratitude we have truly grown" (Fox 1985, 49). When we retell the experiences of teaching/learning as acts of gratitude, not only are we nourished but we are also renewed.

Fourth, we must be present and be a model of this attitude among students. Kessler says, "beyond technique, conceptual understanding, and curriculum, the most effective teaching also includes the quality of our presence – what is commonly called in our profession as modelling" (Kessler 2002, 139). This helps us be more aware of the presence of the Lord with us and of the world around us, including the people we teach. The Bible encourages us to live in the present moment, inviting us to not worry about tomorrow (Matthew 6:34). Living in the present moment helps us recognise God's movement in every aspect of our life and of our professional practice. It will make us more dependent on the Lord and His ways and less dependent on our need to control everything.

### EXERCISE

**Fostering our sense of wonder and practising being in the present moment**

Ask the Lord to increase your awareness to see what is happening around you in the present moment. Have a notebook to regularly write down stories about the progress in learning, change, and transformation you see in your students. Don't underestimate any of these stories, however small they may seem to you. Do not focus on what could have been and was not or on that which has not yet happened. Go over these stories on days when you feel particularly discouraged. Trace the long-term progress. Be amazed by what God is doing here and now and give thanks.

But being present and being models of this attitude also means having an open heart and showing willingness to be vulnerable. It means that we offer students an open window into our own heart, the centre of our soul. Because, as Kessler says: "An open heart is a precondition to being fully present" (Kessler 2002, 142). It is an invitation to allow students to see the work of transformation that the Lord is carrying out in our lives. Being a role model also strengthens the ability to be empathetic with our students, fostering their own vulnerability and openness. Showing empathy and being role models are key instruments that will motivate them towards the transformation of their own hearts.

Fifth, we must be committed to lifelong learning. It is almost funny to think that we sometimes expect the people we teach to learn, but then we do not meet the same standards! There are two fundamental problems with this. On the one hand, it puts our integrity into question: we do not live out what we teach, although we do expect this of our students. That is itself a contradiction and a serious attack on the very heart of education. On the other hand, life and the world evolve, and education needs to keep up. It is not simply a matter of updating our subjects and assignments, but we must also stay abreast of new discoveries in the field of education. This is only possible when we are willing to maintain a humble attitude and be lifelong learners.

We need to see education as something that centres on the student and not on the teacher. This will help us to not fall into subtle traps such as, "I already know this", or, "there is nothing else I want to or can learn". As Christian teachers, ongoing learning really means continuous personal growth. Moreover, education that is centred on the student leads to the idea that students can and must be challenged to seek more learning. One thing that will motivate them to do this is if they see us being committed to a life of continuous learning. When we teach, our motivation should not be to demonstrate how much we know, instead, we should see teaching as an opportunity for shared growth.

Sixth, we must understand and practise *Sabbath* rest. The outside world often has an idyllic view of educational work. The reality is that there is a lot going on behind the scenes: preparation, marking, pastoral care, meetings, etc. Practising *Sabbath* becomes an imperative need for teachers. First, and literally: it is the rest we need to recover physical, mental, and emotional energy, as well as the strength to carry on with a very demanding ministry and profession. But second, we need to understand it in the context of biblical rest. It is important to remember that God rested on the seventh day, and in this way included *Sabbath* as an intentional and integral part of His creation. *Sabbath* is an invitation to refocus on God, to draw new energy from Him. It has to do with being profoundly present before God, enjoying Him and listening to Him, with having our identity in Him be affirmed and refreshed. Campbell writes that: "We cannot give from a dry well, dry land, or a dry empty self" (Campbell 2012, 194-205). *Sabbath* offers us the space we need to respond.

FOOD FOR THOUGHT

- How do you incorporate *Sabbath* into the day-to-day of your ministry?

Finally, we must expose ourselves to a regular assessment process because this provides us with a way to stop and put things into perspective. We can see it as a threat, a way of undermining our role and our teaching abilities, or we can accept it as a positive instrument that acts as a catalyst for and as a channel for growth. In this case, assessment primarily becomes an opportunity for God to examine our character. "Evaluation should be an ongoing process of being aware of what God is doing in our midst and discovering how we can better pursue excellence in training leaders to the glory of God" (Hardy 2012). From this point of view, assessment is an invitation from God to have our hearts open to Him and say, along with the psalmist, "Search me, God, and know my heart; test me and know my anxious thoughts. See if there is any offensive way in me, and lead me in the way everlasting" (Psalm 139:23-24).

## The need for constant renewal

Having said all that, the reality is that teaching has the potential to produce significant fatigue and reasons to be discouraged are constantly lying in wait. Discouragement can be identified at two levels. The first level is related to personal discouragement. We are fallen creatures and, therefore, we continue to deal with sin and spiritual struggles in the midst of our process of transformation. Believers often ask themselves: "Why do we continue to deal with sin if God has already justified us and forgiven us?". This is a subject we have discussed at length in chapter 2, so here we will simply remember that we choose to understand transformation as a journey. In this sense we can say that we have been saved, we are saved now, and we will be saved in the future. As redeemed beings, we become collaborators with God for our transformation, which will be completed in glory: "Everyone must be active in the process of their salvation and transformation to Christlikeness" (Willard 2002, 82). Therefore, this process inevitably includes ups and downs, victories and defeats, obedience and disobedience, light and darkness, sin and repentance. Graham challenges us by saying: "Just as we should accept the limitations and possibilities of our fallen, finite, and redeemed students, we must accept both the limitations and possibilities that result from our own finite, fallen, and redeemed state" (Graham 2009, 114).

Christian teachers, like all other Christians, suffer tensions in our search for a holy life, knowing that it is still a work in progress. Teaching can lead us to all sorts of unbelieving attitudes, which are born from our lack of security in our identity in Christ, a lack of an ability to self-differentiate,[1] and the absence of self-discipline and the ability to renounce oneself. Instead of seeking devotion independence of God, we can seek to fulfil our incomplete desires by the use of power, pride, ego, control, manipulation, roles and titles, etc. However, as Willard says, "life as normally understood, where the object is securing myself, promoting myself, indulging myself, is to be set aside" (Willard 2002, 66). God is inviting us to something more superior and noble: "Self-denial [...] is always the surrender of a lesser dying self for a greater eternal one – the person God intended in creating you" (Willard 2002, 68).

---

[1] Friedman defines a self-differentiated leader as: "Someone who is less likely to become lost in the anxious emotional processes swirling about. I mean someone who can separate while still remaining connected, and therefore can maintain a modifying, non-anxious, and sometimes challenging presence. I mean someone who can manage his or her own reactivity to the automatic receptivity of others, and therefore be able to take stands at the risk of displeasing" (Friedman 2007, 334-344. Kindle version).

The non-self-differentiated leader

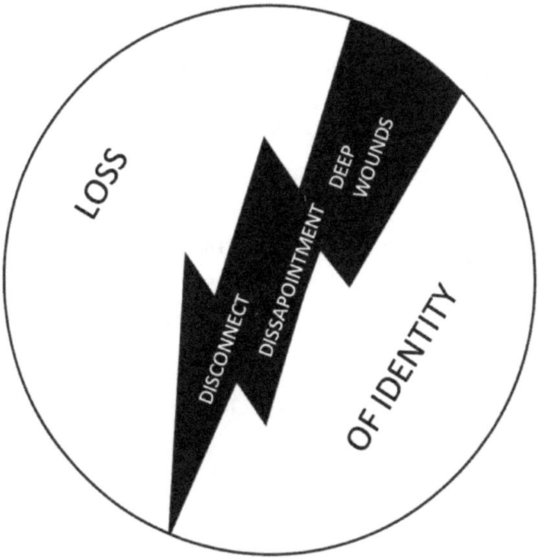


The self-differentiated leader

A second level is related to the intrinsic nature of our vocation. Given that teaching has to do with, as Dress puts it, "entering 'the messy business of human relationships'" (Dress 2012, 28-31), there are all sorts of reasons for discouragement. These difficulties (sometimes) increase because of a lack of clarity and direction, or because of weaknesses within the institutions we serve. Hardy includes other reasons: sacrifice, loneliness, criticism, rejection and enemies, exhaustion, pressure and confusion, lack of stimulation, and the pressure of temptation and failure (Hardy 2012, 5-6). Intrator and Kunzman mention the struggle of: "Keep learning and growing, and how to rekindle the sense of passion and purpose essential for maintaining such growth over the long haul" (Intrator and Kunzman 2006, 38-42).

All these possible reasons for discouragement confirm once more the urgent need to ensure that spiritual renewal is a priority, and to base it on the belief that "[g]ood teaching flows from the identity and integrity of the teacher" (Jackson and Jackson 2002).

## EXERCISE

### A teacher's profile

Write a description of what your profile as a teacher is, using the following guidelines and integrating the content and lessons from this book. Do this exercise with a prayerful attitude, inviting the Lord to be part of this process.

<table>
<tr><td rowspan="4">A teacher's life curve<br>(Significant positive and negative experiences)</td><td>Weaknesses</td><td rowspan="4">Development plan</td><td>Define</td><td rowspan="4">Ongoing assessment</td></tr>
<tr><td></td><td>1. Identity<br>2. Calling/vocation/gifts<br>3. Vision/virtues<br>4. Values</td></tr>
<tr><td>Strengths</td><td>Personal/Ministerial</td></tr>
<tr><td></td><td>1. Use of the Word<br>2. Dependence on the Holy Spirit<br>3. Pedagogical approach<br>4. Pedagogical practices<br>5. Community<br>6. Training others<br>7. Self-care</td></tr>
</table>

**Assessment of the journey so far**

**1. A teacher's life curve**
On a graph, write down any significant positive and negative experiences during your time working as a teacher. Mark them down as a curve, depending on whether it was a positive or negative element.

Analyse the graph:

- Is there anything that catches your attention?
- What carries more weight: the positive experiences or the negative ones? Why do you think this is?
- How does this graph affirm your vocation as a teacher?

**2. Strengths and Weaknesses**
Write down some of the strengths and weaknesses you are aware of about yourself as a teacher. If you want, you could also consult with a friend, a colleague, or a mentor to hear their perspective.

Reflect:

- Is there anything that catches your attention?
- What carries more weight: the positive experiences or the negative ones? Why do you think this is?

**Development plan**

**1. Identity**

Take some time to reflect on and answer the following questions:

- Where do you tend to place your identity as a teacher?
- What are the benefits of this? What are the drawbacks?
- Where does God ask you to place your identity as a teacher?
- What passages from Scripture inspire you to do this?
- Where and when are you more susceptible to compromising your identity as a teacher?
- In one sentence, write down your declaration of identity as a teacher.

**2. Calling/vocation/gifts**

God calls you to Him.
God calls you to participating in what He is doing.
Take some time to reflect on and answer the following questions:

- When did you first feel God's call over your life? A call to ministry? To teaching?
- What are your current feelings regarding this?
- What gifts do you think God has given you? Is teaching one of them? What specific gifts do you think you have as a teacher?
- What legacy do you want to leave behind as a teacher?
- Write down one sentence that represents a ministry declaration that expresses what is in your heart as a teacher.

**3. Vision/virtues**

Take some time to reflect on and answer the following questions, focusing particularly on the type of person/leader/teacher God wants you to be:

- What do you think God wants to really define your relationship with Him?
- How will these truths shape your being?
- What do you think God wants to see in your life regarding virtues and regarding character?
- Write down the crucial virtues you need to be the person God wants you to be.
- Write down the specific ways in which you can cooperate with the Holy Spirit in order to be the person God wants you to be:
    - In your relationships
    - In difficulties
    - In successes
    - In failures
    - In health
    - In suffering
    - In your relationship with the Lord
- What story or teaching from Christ's life illustrates the vision God has for your teaching ministry?
- Write one sentence that represents a declaration of your vision as a teacher.

**4. Values**

Values represent the non-negotiable commitments you need in order to assure your identity, your vocation, and your vision. Remember that these are not doctrinal declarations and they also don't tell you how to carry something out.

· Make a list of 5-7 values that are essential to you as a teacher.
· For each value, write down three measurable goals.
· What impact do you think these values could add to your vocation?

**5. Personal/ministerial**

· Go over the concepts we have developed throughout this book: use of the Word, dependence on the Holy Spirit, pedagogical approach, pedagogical practices, community, training others, and self-care.
· Pray and ask God to show you two concepts He wants you to pay particular attention to.
· Write an action plan for improvement in each of these areas. The plan should include at least three concrete and measurable goals and the time you want to achieve them in.

**Ongoing assessment**

Think about what you will need in order to regularly assess not only your ministerial work as a teacher but also your own spiritual life.

## Conclusion

Even though we have touched on this subject almost at the end of the book, it does not mean that it is a subject that should be moved to the back of the queue of our priorities. Instead of managing crises, and then picking up the pieces and thinking of possible solutions, we should be aiming for prevention. There is a pressing need to look after our spiritual health, but also to constantly and regularly be renewed so that our teaching is truly anointed and has a significant impact on the lives of our students.

# Conclusion

> We all know that what will transform education is not another theory or another book or another formula but a transformed way of being in the world. (Parker 1997, 1)

Dear reader, I hope this book has offered incentive and refreshment for your soul. My desire is that the words have not only led to profound reflections on the ministry of teaching, but that they have also led you to examine your life and your role as a teacher, and to submit these things once more to Christ, who is the author and consummator of our faith, the one who transforms our lives.

My wish is also that this book has been a wake-up call that will not just be about words but that will produce action. Change can generally be quite challenging: we find it hard to change and it is also hard to bring about change in our churches and ministries. To a certain extent, it goes against our very nature and yet it is essential and must be part of our walk with Christ. As this book draws to a close, you may be needing a small extra push that will help you take the first step. Parker Palmer says that teaching should be carried out from a heart full of hope and he challenges us to educational reform, carried out in four stages. In the first stage, the individual makes a personal decision to no longer live divided. Living according to what is in their heart and according to their values is more important than any institutional recognition or action. In the second stage, the individual discovers like-minded people and joins them in order to become part of a support community and to create a space in which to develop their vision. In the third stage, these communities start to have a public impact, even though this makes them be vulnerable and be exposed to criticism. In the fourth stage, they are rewarded for their actions, although not according to the traditional institutional reward system. The reward is knowing that they have lived and acted in line with their vision and values.[1]

The only thing that remains to do is ask you, what step are you going to take to contribute your grain of sand? My own challenge, and one I will

---

[1] You can read more about this in chapter 7 of Palmer Parker's book *The Courage to Teach*.

also set for you, is that some of the things you have read in this book persuade you and that you will be committed to "no longer living divided", and that this will produce changes that impact our ministries, so that we can see people and churches deeply transformed.

I asked my four-year-old son Alex if he could make a drawing to illustrate my book. I told him that the book was about "how to be transformed by Jesus". I left him with a piece of paper and went off to write. When I came home, this is what he presented to me:

When I asked him to explain it to me, he pointed to each element and explained matter-of-factly:

1. The cross (black)
2. Bread (orange)
3. Wine (red)
4. The sun (yellow)
5. Food (blue)
6. Chocolate (brown)
7. Grass (green)
8. Jesus feeding a little girl (purple and yellow)
9. The girl is sad, but then she is happy

I'm not sure whether there is anything else to add... No doubt inspired by the Holy Spirit; I don't think Alex could have illustrated the essence of the book you hold in your hands any more clearly. May the profound truth that Jesus died on the cross for you, for us, be what encourages you to continue travelling the path He has in store for you, knowing that He is with you and that He will bring to completion the work He started (Philippians 1:6). May you know that you are welcome at the table just the way you are. There, we enjoy communion with Him and with each other; there, you are restored and empowered. May you always affirm that "you [Lord] have turned my wailing into dancing" (Psalm 30:11). And may the assurance that God gives you, that His hand is upon you and does not leave you, be the driving force behind your commitment, so that the people whom Jesus has entrusted to you may experience the same as you.

# Bibliography


Aleshire, Daniel O. 2008. *Earthen Vessels: Hopeful Reflections on the Work and Future of Theological Schools.* Grand Rapids, MI: Eerdmans.

Bacote, Vincent, Miguélez C., Laura y Dennis L. Okholm, Eds. 2004. *Evangelicals and Scripture: Tradition, Authority and Hermeneutics.* Downers Grove, IL: InterVarsity Press.

Banks, Robert. 1999. *Reenvisioning Theological Education: Exploring a Missional Alternative to Current Models.* Grand Rapids, MI: Eerdmans.

Cheesman, Graham. 2007. "The Spiritual Formation of Students: A Personal Selection from the Literature". *Theological Education.* http://theologicaleducation.net/articles/download.php?file=The+Spiritual+Formation+of+Students.doc. Accessed on 13 July 2021.

Banks, Robert. 1999. *Paul's Idea of Community*. Peabody, MA: Hendrickson Publishers.

Baumohl, Anton. 1987. *Grow Your Own Leaders.* London: Scripture Union.

Bilezikian, Gilbert. 1997. *Community 101: Reclaiming the Local Church as a Community of Oneness.* Grand Rapids, MI: Zondervan Publishing House.

Bonhoeffer, Dietrich. 1954. *Life Together.* New York, NY: Harper & Row Publishers.

Brown, Jeannine K. 2007. *Scripture as Communication: Introducing Biblical Hermeneutics.* Grand Rapids, MI: Baker Academic.

Cain, Michael Scott. 2001. "Ten Qualities of the Renewed Teacher". *Phi Delta Kappan.* 82:9 (May), 702.

Campbell, Marla. 2012. "Transformational Rest for Educators". *Christian Education Journal.* 9:1 (Spring): 194-205.

Cannell, Linda. 2006. *Theological Education Matters: Leadership Education for the Church.* Newburgh: EDCOT Press.

Cheesman, Graham. 2009. "Theological Education – An Introduction to the Ideas". *Theological Education.* http://theologicaleducation.net/articles/download.php?file=CTE+2+christ+and+training.doc. Accessed on 13 July 2021.

Coe, John. 2000. "Intentional Spiritual Formation in the Classroom: Making Space for the Spirit in the University". *Christian Education Journal.* 4NS, 85-110.

Coljin, Brenda. 2014. "Reading the Bible as Scripture". Class for the course Formational Hermeneutics at Ashland Theological Seminary, Ashland, Ohio, 3 February 2014.

Collinson, Sylvia W. 2004. *Making Disciples: The Significance of Jesus' Educational Methods for Today's Church.* Milton Keynes: Paternoster Press.

Crabb, Larry. 1997. *Connecting: A Radical New Vision.* Nashville, TN: Word.
Downs, Perry G. 1994. *Teaching for Spiritual Growth: An Introduction to Christian Education.* Grand Rapids, MI: Zondervan Publishing House.
Dress, Amelia. 2012. "Reimagining Teacher Development: Cultivating Spirit". *Teacher Development.* January/February, 28-31.
Dunn, James D. G. 1996. *The Epistles to the Colossians and to Philemon. New International Greek Commentary on the NT.* Grand Rapids, MI: Eerdmans Publishing Company. Kindle Edition.
Erickson, Millard. 1983. *Christian Theology.* Grand Rapids, MI: Baker Academic.
Esqueda, Octavio J. 2008, (2nd edition). "God as Teacher". In *The Teaching Ministry of the Church.* Ed. William Yount. Nashville, TN: Broadman and Holman, Nashville, TN.
_______________. 2008, (2nd edition). "The Holy Spirit as Teacher". In *The Teaching Ministry of the Church.* Ed. William Yount. Nashville, TN: Broadman and Holman, Nashville, TN.
_______________. 2008, (2nd edition). "Jesus as Teacher". In *The Teaching Ministry of the Church.* Ed. William Yount. Nashville, TN: Broadman and Holman, Nashville, TN.
Fink, L. Dee. 2012. "A Self-Directed Guide to Designing Courses for Significant Learning". *Theological Education.* http://theologicaleducation.net/articles/view.htm?id=209#sthash.q7ZhlvXY.dpuf. http://theologicaleducation.net/articles/view.htm?id209. Accessed 13 July 2021.
Foster, Richard J. 2010. *Life with God: Reading the Bible for Spiritual Transformation.* New York: HarperCollins. Kindle edition.
Fox, Matthew. 1985. "A Spiritual Renewal of Education". *Tikkun Magazine.* 13:6 (November/December), 49. http://www.tikkun.org/next-gen/a-spiritual-renewal-of-education. Accessed 13 July 2021.
Friedman, Edwin. 2007. *A Failure of Nerve.* New York, NY: Seabury Books. Kindle edition.
Graham, Donovan L. 2009. *Teaching Redemptively: Bringing Grace and Truth into your Classroom.* Colorado Springs, CO: Purposeful Design Publications.
Grainger, David. n. d. "The Mission of God as the Focus for Theological Education". *Biblical Studies.* http://biblicalstudies.org.uk/pdf/ijt/36-1_063.pdf. Accessed 13 July 2021.
Grenz, Stanley J. 1994. *Theology of the Community of God.* Grand Rapids, MI: Eerdmans Publishing Company.
Gundry, Stanley N. Ed. 1987. *Five Views of Sanctification.* Grand Rapids, MI: Zondervan. Kindle edition.
Hardy, Steve. 2012. "Excellence in Teachers". *Theological Education.* http://theologicaleducation.net/articles/view.htm?id=179#sthash.Ret07nS

P%20.dpuf.%20http://theologicaleducation.net/articles/view.htm?id=176. Accessed 13 July 2021.

_______________. 2012. "Excellence in Evaluation and Renewal". *Theological Education.* http://theologicaleducation.net/articles/view.htm?id=181. Accessed 13 July 2021.

Harkness, Allan. 2001. "De-schooling the Theological Seminary: An Appropriate Paradigm for Effective Ministerial Formation". *Theological Education.* http://theologicaleducation.net/articles/download.php?file=Deschooling+theological+ed.pdf. Accessed 13 July 2021.

_______________. 2008. "Assessment in Theological Education: Do our Theological Values Matter?". *Theological Education.* http://theologicaleducation.net/articles/download.php?file=AGH+Assessment+JATE+2008.pdf. Accessed 13 July 2021.

Hendricks, Howard. 2003. *Teaching to Change Lives: 7 Proven Ways to Make Your Teaching Come Alive.* Colorado Springs, CO: Multnomah Books.

Hoekema, Anthony A. 1986. *Created in God's Image.* Exeter: Paternoster Press/Eerdmans.

Hynson, Diana L. 2006. "We love our Teachers". *Clergy Journal.* 82:5 (March), 6-8.

Intrator, Sam, M., and Robert Kunzmann. 2006. "Starting with Soul". *The Educational Forum.* 71:23 (Fall), 38-42. http://www.couragerenewal.org/PDFs/StartingwithSoul.pdf. Accessed 13 July 2021.

Issler, Klaus D. 1996. "Habits of the Excellent Teacher". In *With an Eye on the Future. Development and Mission in the 21st Century: Essays in Honour of Ted W. Ward,* Ed. Duane Elmer and Lois McKinney. Monrovia, CA: MARC Publications.

Jaison, Jessy. "Practical Theology: A Transformative Praxis in Theological Education towards Holistic Formation". *Theological Education.* http://theologicaleducation.net/articles/download.php?file=12+_JOTEAM_Jessy_Jaison.doc. Accessed 13 July 2021.

Johnson, Darrell W. 2002. *Experiencing the Trinity.* Vancouver: Regent College Publishing.

Kelsey, David H. 1992. *To Understand God Truly: What's Theological about a Theological School.* Louisville, KY: John Knox Press.

Kennedy, Declan, Áine Hyland, Norma Ryan. "Writing and Using Learning Outcomes: A Practical Guide". *Theological Education.* http:///theologicaleducation.net/articles/view.htm?id=39. Accessed 13 July 2021.

Kim, Chung-Choon. 1984. "The Contextualization of Theological Education". In *Missions and Theological and Mission in Trialogue,* Eds. Harvie M. Conn and Samuel F. Rowen. Grand Rapids, MI: Zondervan.

Knowles, Malcom S., Elwood F. Holton III and Richard A. Swanson. 2005. *The Adult Learner: The definitive Classic in Adult Education and Human Resource Development.* Burlington, MA: Elsevier.
Kohl, Manfred W. 2009. "Theological Education: What Needs to Be Changed". *Theological Education.* http://theologicaleducation.net/articles/download.php?file=The+Relevance+of+Theological+Education.docx. Accessed 13 July 2021.
Le Bar, Lois. 1958. *Education that is Christian.* Westwood, N.J.: Revell.
Liefield, Walter L. and Linda M. Cannell. 1992. "Spiritual Formation and Theological Education". In *Alive to God: Studies in Spirituality presented to James Houston.* Downers Grove, IL: Intervarsity Press.
_______________. 1991. "The Contemporary Context of Theological Education: A Consideration of Multiple Demands on Theological Educators". *Crux.* 27 (December), 19-27.
McDonald, Glen. 2007. *The Disciplemaking Church: From Dry Bones to Spiritual Vitality.* Grand Haven: FaithWalk.
Marmon, Elle L. 2008. "Teaching as Hospitality". *The Asbury Journal.* 63:2, 33-39.
Nessan, Craig. 2010. "Mission and Theological Education: Berlin, Athens and Tanquebar: North American Perspective". *Mission Studies*. 27, 176-193.
Ninan, Jibu. 2010. "Jesus' Model of Discipling and Its Implications to Theological Education in the 21st Century". *Theological Education.* http://theologicaleducation.net/articles/download.php?file=9+_JOTEAM_Jibu_Ninan.doc. Accessed 13 July 2021.
Nouwen, Henri. 1991. *Creative Ministry.* New York: Double Day.
_______________. 1998. *Reaching Out.* London: Fount Paperbacks, HarperCollins Religious.
Oxenham. 2010. "Competences for Theological Education". European Evangelical Accrediting Association. *Theological Education*. http://theologicaleducation.net/articles/view.htm?id=9. Accessed 13 July 2021.
Palmer, Parker J. 1993. *To Know as we are Known: Education as Spiritual Journey.* New York, NY: HarperCollins Publishers.
_______________. 1997. "The Grace of Great Things: Reclaiming the Sacred in Knowing, Teaching and Learning". http://www.couragerenewal.org/parker/writings/grace-great-things/. Accessed 13 July 2021.
_______________. 1998. "Thirteen Ways of Looking at community (... with a fourteenth thrown in for free)". *The Inner Edge.* (August/September), 1. http://www.couragerenewal.org/parker/writings/13-ways-of-looking-at-community/. Accessed 13 July 2021.
_______________. 1998. *The Courage to Teach: Exploring the Inner Landscape of a Teacher's Life.* San Francisco, CA: Jossey-Bass.

_______________. 2017. *The Courage to Teach Guide for Reflection and Renewal.* San Francisco, CA: Wiley.

_______________. "Community, Conflict, and Ways of Knowing: Ways to Deepen our Educational Agenda". http://www.couragerenewal.org/parker/writings/community-conflict/. Accessed 13 July 2021.

Palmer, Parker J., Megan Scribner and Arthur Zajonc. 2010. *The Heart of Higher Education: A Call to Renewal.* San Francisco, CA: Jossey-Bass.

Pazmiño, Robert W. 1994. "Nurturing the Spiritual Lives of Teachers". In *The Christian Educator's Handbook on Spiritual Formation,* Eds. James C. Wilhoit and Kenneth Gangel, 143-153. Grand Rapids, MI: Baker Books.

_______________. 1998. *Basics of Teaching for Christians: Preparation and Instruction, and Evaluation.* Grand Rapids, MI: Eerdmans Publishing Company.

Peterson, David. 1995. *Possessed by God: A New Testament Theology of Sanctification and Holiness.* Grand Rapids, MI: Eerdmans Publishing Company.

Peterson, Eugene. 1994. *Under the Unpredictable Plant: An Exploration in Vocational Holiness.* Grand Rapids, MI: Eerdmans Publishing Company.

_______________. 1997. "The Seminary as a Place of Spiritual Formation". In *Subversive Spirituality*. Eugene Peterson, 4-60. Grand Rapids, MI: Eerdmans Publishing Company.

_______________. 2011. *Eat This Book: A Conversation in the Art of Spiritual Reading.* London: Hachette UK.

Schafroth, Verena. 2012. "Learner-Centered Quality Management at Theological Seminaries". *Theological Education.* http://theologicaleducation.net/articles/view.htm?id=190. Accessed 13 July 2021.

Shaw, Perry. 2014. *Transforming Theological Education: A Practical Handbook for Integrative Learning.* Carlisle: Langham Global Library.

Siegel, Daniel J. 2011. *Mindsight: Transform your Brain with the New Science of Kindness.* London: Oneworld Publications.

Smith, Gordon. 2010. *Transforming Conversion: Rethinking the Language and Contours of Christian Initiation.* Grand Rapids, MI: Baker Academic.

Smith, David I., James K. A. Smith. Eds. 2001. *Teaching and Christian Practices: Reshaping Faith and Learning.* Grand Rapids, MI: Eerdmans Publishing Company.

Smith, James. 2009. *Desiring the Kingdom: Worship, Worldview, and Cultural Formation.* Grand Rapids, MI: Baker Academic.

TenElshof, Judy. 2001. "Spiritual Formation: How Can Christian Education be Intentional?". *Christian Education Journal.* 4NS (Spring), 111-122.

Universidad Nacional de San Juan. "Verbos para definición de objetivos atendiendo la Taxonomía de Bloom".

http://www.unsj.edu.ar/unsjVirtual/sistema_gestion_calidad/wp-content/uploads/2015/04/Redacciòn-Objetivos-taxonom%C3%ADa-Bloom.P.2.1.9.pdf. Accessed 13 July 2021.

Verghese, Mary. 2010. "Measurable Objectives in Theological Education". *Theological Education. http://theologicaleducation.net/articles/download.php?file=14+_JOTEAM_Mary_Verghese_1.doc.* Accessed 13 July 2021.

Wanak, Lee. 2010. "Towards Perspective Transformation". *Theological Education.* http://theologicaleducation.net/articles/view.htm?id=193. Accessed 13 July 2021.

Wardle, Terry. 2001. *Healing Care, Healing Prayer: Helping the Broken Find Wholeness in Christ.* Abilene, TX: Leafwood Publishers.

________________. 2003. *The Transforming Path: A Christ-Centred Approach to Spiritual Formation.* Abilene, TX: Leafwood Publishers.

________________. 2004. *Outrageous Love, Transforming Power.* Abilene, TX: Leafwood Publishers & ACU Press.

________________. 2015. *Every Breath We Take: Living in the Presence, Love, and Generosity of God.* Abilene, TX: Leafwood Publishers.

Wilhoit, James C. and Linda Rozema. 2005. "Anointed Teaching". CEJ: Series 3, 2:2.

Willard, Dallas. 2002. *Renovation of the Heart: Putting On The Character of Christ.* UK edition. Nottingham: IVP.

Wingate, Andrew. 2005. "Overview of the History of the Debate about Theological Education". *International Review of Mission.* 94:373, 235-247.

Witherington, Ben, III. 2005. "Retelling the story of Post-Modernity". In *Cultivating a Thoughtful Faith,* Eds. Maxie D. Dunham and Steve G. W. Moore, 37-49. Nashville, TN: Abingdon Press.

Zuck, Roy B. 1998. *Spirit-Filled Teaching: The Power of the Holy Spirit in Your Ministry*. Nashville, TN: World Publishing.